Study Guide

Marketing

Study Guide

▶ Vicki Griffis

Marketing

second edition

▶ **Warren J. Keegan**
Pace University, New York City and Westchester

▶ **Sandra E. Moriarity**
University of Colorado at Boulder

▶ **Thomas R. Duncan**
University of Colorado at Boulder

Prentice Hall
Englewood Cliffs, New Jersey 07632

Production editor: Lynne Breitfeller
Assistant editor: Melissa Steffans
Production coordinator: Ken Clinton

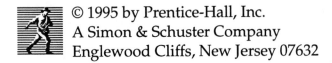 © 1995 by Prentice-Hall, Inc.
A Simon & Schuster Company
Englewood Cliffs, New Jersey 07632

Printed in the United States of America

10   9   8   7   6   5   4   3   2   1

ISBN   0-13-125956-3

Prentice-Hall International (UK) Limited, *London*
Prentice-Hall of Australia Pty. Limited, *Sydney*
Prentice-Hall Canada Inc., *Toronto*
Prentice-Hall Hispanoamericana, S.A., *Mexico*
Prentice-Hall of India Private Limited, *New Delhi*
Prentice-Hall of Japan, Inc., *Tokyo*
Simon & Schuster Asia Pte. Ltd., *Singapore*
Editora Prentice-Hall do Brasil, Ltda., *Rio de Janeiro*

CONTENTS

USING THE STUDY GUIDE

This study guide was developed for the textbook, <u>Marketing</u> 2/e, by Keegan, Moriarty and Duncan. The guiding philosophy of the study guide is to provide some tools for students to increase their understanding of the marketing concepts presented in the textbook. It is recommended that you read the text chapter in its entirety. Once finished, you should review the vocabulary terms. You should then be ready to work the applications project for that particular chapter. The final review of a chapter should be the completion of the practice questions.

This study guide will NOT serve as a replacement for your textbook. It will NOT provide a shortcut to learning. What it will do is give you the opportunity to fully comprehend the concepts presented. It will allow you to experiment with the application of marketing concepts to practical situations in a relatively risk-free setting. Learning requires practice, which means mistakes will be made. The intention here is to allow you to learn now, before your mistakes incur larger penalties.

<u>APPLICATION PROJECTS</u> are included for Chapters 1-21. Concepts from chapter 22 are included in the marketing plan project for chapter four. The *purpose* for each project refers to a chapter objective. You will find it helpful to refer to the corresponding section of the chapter while working on the project. The projects are designed to improve your understanding, not test your ability to memorize. You will find the marketing concepts easier to learn once you understand how they can be used. Because many of the projects are based on personal evaluation, there are not clear cut "answers". The correct solution is the one that most closely implements the relevant marketing concept based on the given parameters.

<u>PRACTICE QUESTIONS</u> are included for all 22 chapters. For each chapter there are 15 comprehesion/definition questions and 15 applications-oriented questions. The comprehension/definition questions will test your knowledge of the marketing concepts and principles presented in the chapter. The applications questions will expand your knowledge to include the ability to "fit" a concept with a situation. If your instructor allows you the opportunity for exam feedback, investigate the type of question that gives you the most difficulty. Spend more time studying the concepts and vocabulary in the chapter, if you find the definition questions are most difficult. If the applications questions give you trouble, focus on the examples/boxes in the text and form a study group to discuss concepts.

As we near the 21st century, marketing principles will be integrated into every facet of business. You will need to understand their meaning and application to generate success in your career--and even more importantly to contribute to an improved standard of living globally. Good Luck.   V.B.G.

Study Guide

Marketing

CHAPTER ONE
APPLICATIONS PROJECT

Purpose: To understand the impact and evolution of marketing philosophy.

Instructions: Using <u>The Body Shop</u> case in the back of your textbook, examine the societal marketing concept in action. Discuss potential differences in The Body Shop's method of doing business under each of the different philosophies.

<u>Production-oriented:</u>

<u>Sales-oriented:</u>

<u>Marketing Driven:</u>

Instructions: Consumerism is the impetus behind many socially responsible business actions. Which consumer groups and/or issues would be particularly relevant to <u>The Body Shop</u>? List four and briefly discuss their impact.

1.

2.

3.

4.

CHAPTER ONE
EXAM PRACTICE QUESTIONS

The following questions are designed to test your comprehension of marketing concepts and terminology.

1. A marketing transaction in which a buyer gives something of value to a seller in return for a product that the buyer values is called a(n)
A. transatorium.
B. issuance.
C. distribution channel.
D. price relationship.
E. exchange.

2. A market is
A. a group of products.
B. everyone who goes to a market to buy food.
C. all the people who know about a particular product.
D. everyone who understands marketing.
E. all the people who want or need a particular product and might buy it.

3. People who buy products for their own personal use or for the use of others in their household are generally referred to as a(n)
A. industrial market.
B. consumer market.
C. institutional market.
D. personal market.
E. user market.

4. Goods which are used up fairly quickly and thus purchased frequently are called:
A. durable good.
B. plain goods.
C. quick goods.
D. expendable goods.
E. consumables.

5. According to the concept of supply and demand, demand is
A. how much each person desires of a particular product.
B. the amount that buyers would be willing to purchase at a particular price.
C. the amount that sellers are willing to offer for sale.
D. the total amount of goods manufactured by a company.
E. the total amount of goods bought by a particular consumer.

6. How are needs different from wants?
A. Needs are how consumers seek to satisfy wants.
B. Wants are how consumers seek to satisfy needs.
C. Wants are the basis for needs.
D. Needs are smaller than wants.
E. They mean the same thing; they aren't different.

7. The societal marketing philosophy is an approach which holds that
A. firms should hold parties for all society people.
B. societal methods should be used in all advertising.
C. firms should maintain or improve the well-being of society.
D. firms should compete with societal competitors.
E. everyone should be treated equally.

8. Dentists and auto mechanics provide a(n) _____ to consumers.
A. consumable good
B. durable good
C. market
D. service
E. idea

9. The approach to marketing which focuses on the persuasive strengths of personal selling is the
A. marketing concept.
B. social responsibility.
C. sales-oriented.
D. mass marketing.
E. demand.

10. The marketing mix
A. consists of product, place, push, and pull.
B. is an uncontrollable business factor.
C. is controlled by accounting.
D. consists of price, finance, accounting, and distribution.
E. consists of product, price, distribution, and promotion.

11. A product
A. must be tangible.
B. is anything that can satisfy a need or want.
C. is what the consumer sees.
D. must be a good or service.
E. is described by all of the above.

12. Which of the following statements about marketing is FALSE?
A. Marketing affects almost every part of our daily life.
B. Marketing offers many rewarding career opportunities.
C. Marketing is only advertising.
D. Marketing is vital for economic growth and development.
E. Marketing concepts and techniques apply for nonprofit organizations--as well as for profit-seeking organizations.

13. The marketing philosophy approaches profitability as
A. a by-product of satisfying customer's wants.
B. the end result of increasing volume.
C. having a longer horizon than the next quarterly statement.
D. not really necessary if the customer's needs are being met.
E. developing a lean organization that can produce new products quickly which can aid profitability.

14. The broad function of marketing is to
A. make advertising believable.
B. support the economic welfare of the country.
C. bring buyer and seller together.
D. bring quality products to the market.
E. see to it that products are transported to the market.

15. The ratio of benefits/cost is referred to in marketing as
A. promotion
B. positioning
C. price
D. value
E. need

The remaining questions are designed to evaluate your ability to apply the text concepts.

16. Caustic Cola has decided that everyone in the world will like their new spicy cola. They most likely will try to appeal to a
A. mass market.
B. niche market.
C. sellers market.
D. trend market.
E. industrial market.

17. Martin's company bought a computer for Martin to use in his job as an accountant with the company. Martin's company is functioning as part of the
A. consumer market.
B. reseller market.
C. bonus market.
D. sellers market.
E. industrial market.

18. A small Massachusetts company names Instron was able to recoup development costs on a specialized ceramics testing machine by selling its product to customers in Japan, Europe, Taiwan, and China, as well as the United States. They achieved profits partially because the increase volume of sales from selling globally created
A. additional value.
B. higher prices.
C. economies of scale.
D. better quality control.
E. easier marketing.

19. ABC corporation spends thousands of dollars each year on sophisticated research to find out what its customers and potential consumers want. The company then disseminates this information and assigns department managers the job of finding ways to meet the needs of these consumers. This company is using
A. the promotion concept.
B. the 4 P's approach.
C. the consumption approach.
D. the invention approach.
E. the marketing concept.

20. The salesman who sells most of the bakery equipment to Continental Baking visits the plant frequently and attempts to develop a perceived partnership with the plant manager. The salesman is practicing
A. aggressive public relations.
B. partnership prospecting.
C. premium development.
D. relationship marketing.
E. sales incentives.

21. Managers at XYZ Corporation decided that more emphasis was needed this year on developing new products and product improvements and less on aggressive advertising programs. The managers are working at managing the firm's
A. marketing mission.
B. promotion package.
C. production efficiencies.
D. marketing mix.
E. financial program.

22. IBM's strategy to use personal selling by IBM's sales force to large customers and through heavy advertising to smaller customers concerns what part of the marketing mix?
A. promotion (marketing communications)
B. place (distribution)
C. product
D. positioning
E. public relations

23. Ben and Jerry's Homemade Inc. operates solar powered vans and maintains voter registration facilities in all its Vermont ice cream parlors. This practices are examples of using
A. marketing myopia.
B. a mass marketing approach.
C. a specialized promotion program.
D. a 4 P's approach.
E. a societal marketing philosophy.

24. H&R Blocks tax advice and Jenny Craig's weight loss guidance to consumers are types of
A. promotion.
B. product.
C. place.
D. consumable.
E. package.

25. All of the following are consumable goods EXCEPT
A. eyeglasses.
B. chewing gum.
C. breakfast cereal.
D. coffee.
E. dog biscuits.

26. The "market" for a four year university
A. consists soley of those students currently enrolled.
B. only includes incoming freshman.
C. includes most high school seniors.
D. consists soley of high school seniors.
E. consists soley of only university alumni.

27. Ralph's Marine repair has determined their best target market to be owners of boats under 25' with inboard engines living within a 20 mile radius of their shop. This target group would be considered a(n)
A. niche market.
B. sellers market.
C. mass market.
D. industrial market.
E. reseller market.

28. The ability and willingness of Keebler to produce consumer goods creates
A. demand.
B. supply.
C. production.
D. exchange.
E. transaction.

29. According to Maslow's theory, social needs are satisfied
A. with membership in group activities.
B. through an appreciation of value.
C. with a niche market.
D. in a socially responsible chain letter.
E. with supply side economics.

30. Eric bought an apple from the bookstore to munch in the break between classes. He was functioning as part of the
A. institutional market.
B. sellers market.
C. industrial market.
D. consumer market.
E. bonus market.

CHAPTER TWO
APPLICATIONS PROJECT

Purpose: To increase understanding of the application of Total Quality Management practices.

Instructions: Using normal flow chart symbols, diagram the registration process at your school. Be sure to indicate all decision trees and alternate choices.

Example:

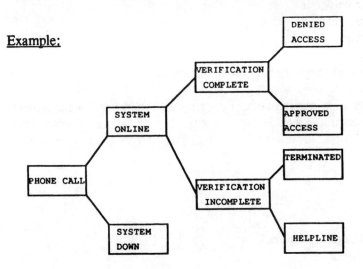

Instructions: After you have completed your flow chart, highlight the areas that are critical to meeting customer expectations. Try to apply a Total Quality Management philosophy to these potential "hotspots." Based on your blueprint, what suggestions would you make to your registrar's office to deliver quality customer service?

Hot Spots	Suggestions
1.	
2.	
3.	
4.	
5.	
6.	

The following questions are designed to test your comprehension of marketing concepts and terminology.

1. A "marketing philosophy" organizational model differs from a traditional model in that
A. marketing is not a department.
B. sales and marketing are separate.
C. marketing interfaces with all other functional areas.
D. the head of marketing is a VP.
E. the accounting department reports through the marketing department.

2. Confusion over who has final decision making authority - a product manager from a project team or functional manager - often occurs in a
A. vertical organization.
B. franchise organization.
C. centralized organization.
D. intrapreneurial enterprise.
E. matrix system of organization.

3. The advantages of a centralized organization include
A. increased flexibility in new markets.
B. more responsibility in SBU's.
C. more initiative for individual managers.
D. more control and increased efficiency.
E. improved employee moral.

4. Consensus management is a form of
A. decentralized organization structure.
B. dual management system structure.
C. centralized organization structure.
D. leader-based management system.
E. hierarchical organizational structure.

5. A brand manager is
A. a product manager who focuses on a specific brand.
B. a sales representative who makes recommendations for new brands.
C. a product development manager who works primarily on one brand.
D. a marketing manager whose job it is to develop brand awareness for the company.
E. the public relations director assigned to building brand image.

6. The corporate culture of a company is
A. the ethnic makeup of the company's employees.
B. the corporate strategy.
C. the attitude of the chief executive officer.
D. a pattern of shared values and beliefs.
E. the geographic culture in which the company is based. (e.g., the U.S.)

7. Stakeholders are
A. the principles which support the organization.
B. any organization or individual who provides financing for a company.
C. any group or individual who can affect, or be affected by, an organization.
D. the product managers and brand leaders who direct the matrix system.
E. the tenets of the corporate mission statement.

8. A strategic business unit is
A. company division that operates independently as a profit center.
B. consulting firm which specializes in marketing strategies.
C. department responsible for marketing strategies for a corporation.
D. company which incorporates a 10-year strategic planning process.
E. firm which uses the BCG strategic planning matrix.

9. A key advantage of centralized management is
A. flexibility.
B. market responsiveness.
C. improved moral.
D. increased control.
E. all of the above.

10. The TQM view of marketing's place in the organization
A. is a separate independent department.
B. is a replacement for accounting.
C. is an integrated philosophy being practiced throughout all departments.
D. is the control department for quality.
E. is nonexistent, with TQM there is no need for marketing principles to be practiced.

11. A corporate mission statement describes the company's
A. brand management.
B. marketing tactics.
C. formal business values.
D. personnel policies.
E. profit and loss position.

12. The concept of marketing myopia means
A. that firms are too focused on consumers needs and fail to make a profit.
B. that a firm is too focused on their product and not focused enough on consumer   needs.
C. that firms are too focused on sales that they forget about their products.
D. that firms think too far ahead and fail to make a profit
E. that firms ignore corporate culture and ultimately go out of business

13. Programs that maximize quality, like Total Quality Management (TQM), are really directed at creating
A. profit.
B. new product innovation.
C. revenue.
D. customer satisfaction.
E. sales.

14. Which of the following is TRUE in "boundary-less organizations"?
A. marketing activities are isolated
B. walls exist between functional areas
C. finance is the key "boundary-spanning" unit.
D. people who handle marketing activities are more likely to interface with other areas.
E. all of the above are true

15. Which of the following is NOT a component of corporate culture?
A. attitude toward risk taking
B. a pattern of shared values
C. attitude toward innovation
D. inventory turnover ratio
E. long term-vs-short term thinking

The remaining questions are designed to evaluate your ability to apply the text concepts.

16. GE has thirteen different divisions, each with its own marketing strategy, position and responsibility for profits. Divisions include, for example, aircraft engines, appliances, lighting and medical systems. These divisions could be called
A. corporate partitions.
B. strategic business units.
C. marketing development units.
D. corporate functional departments.
E. traditional unit environments.

17. At Illinois Tool Works, managers of SBU's create their own marketing plans, and spin off new SBU's whenever employees invent a new product. This company is a good example of a company using
A. centralized approach.
B. highly structured approach.
C. decentralized approach.
D. dual management structure.
E. invention operations structure.

18. As the executive vice president of marketing, Elaine is in the _____ category on the organizational chart.
A. upper management
B. staff
C. product manager
D. brand manager
E. specialist

19. "To safely deliver a hot pizza in 30 minutes or less at a fair and a reasonable profit" was Dominos'
A. marketing plan.
B. statement of intent.
C. corporate mission statement.
D. advertising tactical program.
E. company marketing program.

20. Windex lost market share to rival Glass Plus because it did not recognize that consumers were using their products for more than just cleaning windows. In other words, the company lost touch with consumer needs. Ted Levitt and other marketing experts would call this
A. marketing focus.
B. marketing myopia.
C. corporate colossus.
D. window orientation.
E. sales orientation.

21. Dell Computer sells hardware made by other companies, sells direct to its customers, and has a large staff of well-informed sales reps who can answer customers' questions. Dell is an example of what your book would call a
A. marketing organization.
B. second-hand dealer.
C. sales franchise.
D. retail superstore.
E. wholesale hypermarket.

22. Gus works as a promotions manager at Smith Manufacturing. He reports directly to the director of the marketing department as well as to four product managers who head up product teams on which he serves. Smith Manufacturing is using a
A. vertical organization structure.
B. centralized organization structure.
C. matrix system of organization.
D. dual integration system.
E. mixed hierarchy organization.

23. Jan has a new idea for a toy for three to five year olds. She decides to produce some samples and market them through craft fairs and flea markets. Jan would be considered a(n)
A. entrepreneur.
B. intrapreneur.
C. extrapreneur.
D. brand manager.
E. bureaucrat.

24. A scientist at 3M developed the idea for the successful 3M product post-it notes. He was given resources and encouragement to develop his product idea while at work. He would be considered a(n)
A. product manager.
B. entrepreneur.
C. intrapreneur.
D. extrapreneur
E. marketing manager.

25. Bob works for the local junior college, his daughter takes classes there and his wife is a member of the Board of Trustees. According to TQM, they would be considered
A. customers.
B. stakeholders.
C. SBU's.
D. entrepreneur.
E. marketers.

26. GE has 13 separate profit centers each with their own marketing strategy. These are called
A. strategic business units.
B. matrix models.
C. quality circles.
D. BCG's
E. product managers

27. Disney's _____ is "to provide entertainment to children of all ages".
A. corporate culture
B. marketing tactic
C. marketing myopia
D. brand management
E. mission statement

28. For most companies, the "total quality approach" demands
A. complete ignorance of stakeholder needs.
B. a complete shift in corporate culture.
C. a total focus on profit.
D. static, centralized management.
E. short-term thinking.

29. Which of the following is an internal corporate factor that affects marketing?
A. aging population
B. national political climate
C. trade deficits
D. employee expertise
E. shifting demographics

30. The primary organizational issues facing marketing personnel in global firms are
A. appropriate degree of centralization.
B. how to manage conflicts between cultures.
C. brand management authority.
D. corporate restructuring.
E. all of the above.

CHAPTER THREE
APPLICATIONS PROJECT

Purpose: To increase understanding of the ways in which the sociological, industrial, and technological environments shape a firm's external marketing environment.

Instructions: Using The Body Shop integrative case in the back of your text, analyze the threats and opportunities in their external marketing environment. Place a (+) for opportunity or a (-) for a threat to the left of each variable. Indicate the condition of the variable on the right. The outline is provided as a comprehensive reminder of the scope of the external environment.

Example: (-) *Business cycle: Recession*

Economic Environment
Economic system:
   free market, controlled, mixed

Economic cooperation:

Economic growth:

Business cycle:

Inflation:

Purchasing power:

Foreign exchange:

Competitive Environment
Market share:

Competitive structure:
   monopoly, oligopoly, perfect competition, monopolistic competition

Legal and Regulatory Environment
Laws:

Regulations:

Self-regulation:

Consumer protection measures:

Trade policy:

Other:

Sociocultural Environment
Demographics:

Threat of ethnocentrism:

Other:

Industry Environment
Growth:

Price trends:

Stage in product life cycle:

Other:

Technological Environment
Place of change:

Industry specific impact:

CHAPTER THREE
EXAM PRACTICE QUESTIONS

The following questions are designed to test your comprehension of marketing concepts and terminology.

1. A firm's external marketing environment is
A. the factors and forces outside the organization that shape markets.
B. the firm's marketing mix.
C. the firm's infrastructure and management marketing philosophy.
D. the external marketing orientation.
E. the environment which shapes the markets outside the firm's home country.

2. A chance to create value for customers at a profit is known as
A. an opportunity.
B. a creation.
C. a value-added position.
D. a threat.
E. an external marketing environment.

3. The primary purpose of the North American Fair Trade Agreement (NAFTA) is to
A. eliminate barriers to trade and investment among the U.S., Mexico, and Canada.
B. consolidate the governments of North America into one government.
C. be sure that North American countries trade freely with the rest of the world.
D. provide a more open market in South America for North American products.
E. create a more open trade agreement with Europe and Japan.

4. A period of low economic growth when unemployment levels rise ant the rate of increase in income and purchasing power slows is called
A. a recession
B. instability
C. economic reprisal
D. a depression
E. inflation

5. Exchange rates:
A. are controlled by markets.
B. are the value of a country's currency in another country.
C. equal the availability amount of hard currency in a nation.
D. do not fluctuate.
E. are a country's balance of trade.

6. An international marketer has to understand that different countries have different underlying value systems and resulting in different
A. technological environments.
B. envirological environments.
C. psychoeconomic environme.nts
D. sociocultural environments.
E. econosystems.

7. A monopoly differs from monopolistic competition primarily in the
A. number of buyers in the market.
B. product quantities provided.
C. number of sellers in the market.
D. degree of differentiation among buyers.
E. demand for the products offered.

8. When wages and prices rise without an increase in productivity, the result is
A. discretionary income.
B. inflation.
C. GNP.
D. a balance of trade.
E. depression.

9. The primary purpose of the European Community (EC) is to
A. block trade.
B. reduce exports.
C. establish free movement of goods, services, capital, and people in Europe.
D. guarantee free movement of capital globally.
E. control the Pacific Rim.

10. An increase in a nation's gross national product is considered
A. economic growth.
B. free trade.
C. a technological opportunity.
D. inflation.
E. a recession.

11. The marketing environment for an organization consists of
A. the political environment.
B. the technological environment.
C. sociological trends.
D. competitors marketing mix variables.
E. all of the above.

12. The Pure Food and Drug Act and the Fair Packaging and Labelling Act would be considered part of an organizations _____ environment.
A. competitive
B. technological
C. sociocultural
D. political
E. economic

13. The practice of relaxing or eliminating laws governing specific industries is called
A. privatization.
B. nationalization.
C. deregulation.
D. trade policy.
E. demographics.

14. As part of the sociocultural environment, _____ includes predominantly quantifiable data such as age, gender, race, income, and education.
A. geographics
B. technologics
C. economic system
D. privatization
E. demographics

15. A recession
A. can present a threat to some marketers and an opportunity for others.
B. always follows a depression.
C. necessitated the passing of the Sherman Act.
D. is a period of economic growth.
E. reduces unemployment.

The remaining questions are designed to evaluate your ability to apply the text concepts.
16. In Cuba and North Korea, the government owns most of the manufacturing facilities and makes decisions about how much of different products will be produced. These two countries are the last two examples in the world of
A. free-market systems.
B. sociocultural systems.
C. economic equity systems.
D. economic enterprise systems.
E. controlled-market systems.

17. Which of the following is the most likely use of discretionary income?
A. to pay for a vacation
B. to pay taxes
C. to pay rent
D. to buy food
E. to purchase medical insurance

18. The invention of the facsimile machine has created wonderful opportunities for fax machine manufacturers, while it represents a major threat to Federal Express and the U.S. Postal Service. This is a good example of how both opportunities and threats can be present by changes in the
A. technological environment.
B. econocultural environment.
C. demographic environment.
D. communigraphic environment.
E. allocation environment.

19. Del Monte introduced a Fruit Cup product with single servings of fruit in a can in part to respond to the increase in single adults in the population. This is an example of how marketers adapt to changes in the
A. technological environment.
B. econocultural environment.
C. demographical environment.
D. sociolinguistic environment.
E. popugraphic environment.

20. Throughout the Eastern Block, businesses which had been state-owned are being transferred or sold to private enterprise. This process is called
A. deregulation.
B. corporatization.
C. easternization.
D. state abolition.
E. privatization.

21. The National Advertising Review Council (NARC) consists of various companies who monitor their and other companies' advertisements. This group could be considered
A. the enforcement agency for the Food and Drug Administration.
B. the management arm of the National Advertising Association.
C. the self-regulatory arm of the advertising industry.
D. the legal environment for the advertising industry.
E. the sociocultural nemesis of advertisers.

22. When the state of Idaho branded its potatoes, it basically moved from
A. monopoly to oligopoly.
B. perfect competition to monopolistic competition.
C. monopolistic competition to monopoly.
D. oligopoly to perfect competition.
E. perfect competition to oligopoly.

23. Which of the following industries is the best example of an oligopoly?
A. fresh fruits and vegetables
B. long-distance telephone service
C. public utilities
D. gasoline retailing
E. direct marketing

24. The aging of the population and decreasing size of families proposes an environmental _____ to Disney World's Magic Kingdom.
A. political weakness
B. sociological threat
C. technological strength
D. competitor
E. price structure

25. Cathy paid her taxes and all household expenses, with the money she had left she bought a boat. The purchase money would be considered
A. discretionary income.
B. inflation.
C. real income.
D. GNP.
E. the exchange rate

26. While traveling through Europe, Russ lost money everytime he transferred his money into the currency of the host country. This is due to
A. entrance fees.
B. foreign exchange rates.
C. tariffs.
D. currency trading rates.
E. balance of trade

27. Hertz, Avis, and Budget Rent-a-Car are all part of each other's _____ environment.
A. political
B. sociocultural
C. stakeholder
D. consumer
E. competitive

28. Hershey and M&M Mars dominate the candy industry. Together their sales account for approximately 70% of industry sales. This is called their
A. company positioning.
B. monopoly.
C. revenue reach.
D. market share.
E. customer ratio.

29. Laundry soap, cat food and soft drinks all operate in a competitive environment known as a(n)
A. oligopoly.
B. monopolistic competition.
C. monopoly.
D. monolith.
E. pedagogy.

30. Your local utility company is an example of
A. monopoly.
B. oligopoly.
C. electropoly.
D. soliloque.
E. perfect competition.

CHAPTER FOUR
APPLICATIONS PROJECT

Purpose: To gain experience developing a marketing plan.

Instructions: Using the following marketing plan outline, develop a marketing plan for a product you believe in--yourself. Analyze the external opportunities and threats confronting you in the job market in the Situation Analysis (II). Evaluate the degree of importance and your level of expertise for each of the categories listed. In Career Objectives (III), state your short and long-term career goals in measurable terms. Then let Strategy (IV), guides you through a plan of action based on your own personal strengths and weaknesses. All successful marketers know the importance of feedback. Evaluation (V) provides a check list to compare your objectives to your actual results to discover additional areas of improvement.

II. Situation Analysis (External environmental influences)

   A. Political/Legal

       1. Licenses required

       2. Professional associations in your industry

   B. Socio/Cultural

       1. Age trends

       2. Multicultural significance

       3. Professional appearance/manner

       4. Business etiquette

   C. Economic

       1. Salary range

       2. Present value vs future value tradeoffs

       3. Opportunity costs

       4. Cost/Benefit analysis

D. Technology

    1. Technical skills

    2. Computer literacy

III. Career Objectives

A. Short range

    1. Quality of life

    2. Benefits/Salary

    3. Values

B. Long range

    1. Career potential

    2. Salary/Benefits

    3. Societal impact

IV. Strategy

A. Employment Prospects

    1. Ranked by priority

    2. References

B. Product - YOU

    1. Differential advantages

    2. Summary of qualifications

C. Price

    1. Acceptable salary

    2. Negotiable benefits

D. Distribution

    1. Geographic preference

    2. Willingness to relocate

E. Promotion

    1. Resume Mailings

    2. Networking opportunities

        a. professional associations

    3. Employment Agency representation

V. Evaluation

A. Short range

    1. Compare your Strategy (IV) with your peers to determine your competitive advantage

    2. Share your marketing plan with career counselors to get their input on feasibility and potential for success.

B. Long range

    1. Conduct a one-year check against your objectives.

    2. Compare progress in 5 year intervals.

CHAPTER FOUR
EXAM PRACTICE QUESTIONS

The following questions are designed to test your comprehension of marketing concepts and terminology.

1. Deciding which strategic business units to keep, which to shut down, and if the company should start or buy new units is an important function of
A. long-range corporate planning.
B. marketing plans.
C. strategic orientation.
D. business economic strategies.
E. corporate mission analysis.

2. A fiscal year is
A. a year in which record sales levels are achieved.
B. a year when a company is in the red.
C. an examination of annual growth patterns.
D. the first 12-month period after a new product or business is launched.
E. a 12-month period which the company uses for its corporate planning.

3. Short-term, specific actions which describe how the plan will be executed are called
A. strategies.
B. objectives .
C. tactics.
D. rationales.
E. business executions.

4. A marketing plan is
A. a statement of financial objectives and resource allocation strategies.
B. a corporate mission statement.
C. a document that outlines the major decisions that will guide marketing efforts.
D. a description of marketing tactics.
E. a discussion of the company's promotion plans.

5. According to your text, a firm's competitive advantage is
A. its ability or willingness to do something better than its competition.
B. its financial status relative to its competitors.
C. its confidential information about a competitor.
D. its focus on the competitor.
E. the competitive review stage of the SWOT analysis.

6. Target markets are
A. focus groups.
B. groups of likely customers on whom a company focuses marketing efforts.
C. groups of competitors targeted by a company for direct challenges.
D. product categories determined to be best for expansion.
E. target consumers selected for a marketing survey.

7. A pull strategy involves
A. selling a product primarily to the trade.
B. selling dental extraction products.
C. leveraging extra resources through competitive advantage.
D. use of consumer-focused marketing to create a demand for products.
E. pulling in market share with aggressive selling to retailers.

8. Establishing the way a brand ranks or compares to the competition in consumer's minds is called
A. brand establishment.
B. competitive challenge.
C. positioning.
D. trademarking.
E. mind communication.

9. Portfolio analysis
A. requires separate income statements for each item included.
B. requires comprehension of the internal strengths and weaknesses of the strategic business units.
C. does not include external market factors.
D. required by the FTC.
E. can only be conducted internally.

10. The Boston Consulting Group (BCG) Matrix
A. is a tool for portfolio analysis.
B. uses nine levels of analysis.
C. is based solely on sales.
D. analyzes an organization's stock portfolio.
E. is described by all of the above.

11. Strategic planning is
A. concerned with a 12 month time period.
B. used by successful companies to chart a long range course of action.
C. not applicable to non-profit companies.
D. focused on tactics, not objectives.
E. a replacement for a marketing plan.

12. Which market growth strategy expands sales through increasing consumption from existing customers?
A. market expansion
B. market development
C. market positioning
D. market segmenting
E. market penetration

13. The focus of a market diversification growth strategy is on
A. existing markets and new products.
B. new markets and new products.
C. new markets and existing products.
D. existing markets and existing products.
E. existing markets and new brands.

14. Which of the following is NOT part of the marketing mix?
A. price
B. product
C. planning
D. promotion
E. distribution

15. Marketing communication plans
A. are developed as part of promotion.
B. do not need objectives.
C. are best measured using sales growth.
D. add value through product modification.
E. are developed before the strategic plan.

The remaining questions are designed to evaluate your ability to apply the text concepts.

16. Millennium batteries are now number one in the rapidly growing rechargeable battery market. The Boston Consulting Group (BCG) matrix would classify this product as a
A. dog.
B. star.
C. cash cow.
D. question mark.
E. pig.

17. Environmental concerns allow Millennium to effectively differentiate themselves by promoting that their batteries are reusable. These environmental concerns would most likely be viewed by Millennium as representing an
A. external opportunity.
B. internal strength.
C. external threat.
D. internal opportunity.
E. internal weaknesses.

18. When Marla went to the store, she planned on buying a box of Quaker Instant Grits with real butter flavor that she had seen advertised in Southern Living. When she couldn't find the product, she asked the store manager to stock it for her. This is an example of the result of a
A. push strategy.
B. intercept strategy.
C. tiered strategy.
D. pull strategy.
E. SWOT strategy.

19. Kimberly Clark's aggressive use of coupons, price discounts, and direct mail are good examples of use of a strategy of
A. market creation.
B. market development.
C. market penetration.
D. market expansion.
E. market diversification.

20. "To create a 25% level of brand awareness among the target audience in North America through the use of a highly visible advertising campaign" would be a
A. marketing communication tactic.
B. marketing communication strategy.
C. marketing communication objective.
D. distribution objective.
E. distribution strategy.

21. Which element of the marketing mix is affected by the use of vending machines to rent video tapes?
A. distribution
B. product
C. price
D. direct marketing
E. marketing communication

22. Harley Davidson's move into motorcycle clothing and accessories as described in the integrative case represents which market growth strategy?
A. market development
B. market penetration
C. global penetration
D. market diversification
E. product penetration

23. Subway has announced they plan to move up to the number two position in the still rapidly growing fast food market. This means that currently they would be classified as a _____ on the BCG matrix.
A. star
B. donkey
C. question mark
D. cash cow
E. dog

24. In the cosmetics industry, the "natural/eco-friendly" product line is experiencing high growth. The Body Shop has been the market leader and innovator of these products since they began. Where would you categorize them on the BCG matrix?
A. bird
B. star
C. cash cow
D. question mark
E. dog

25. Why is "to increase market share" NOT a good marketing objective?
A. no focus on profit
B. it ignores sales
C. it uses an externally impacted criteria
D. it is impossible to measure and evaluate
E. it is too rigid

26. A SWOT analysis for The Body Shop would include
A. the opportunities created by a reduction in export taxes.
B. the threats of internal management conflict.
C. the weaknesses evident in the aging of Americans.
D. the internal strengths created by The Body Shop's brand equity.
E. A and D

27. Which of the following would NOT be included in marketing planning for Saturn?
A. description of target market
B. GM's corporate mission statement
C. sales/market share objectives
D. procedures for collecting feedback on owner satisfaction
E. competitive pricing research on other midsize cars

28. When Anheuser Busch introduced O'Douls non alcoholic beer, they intensified personal selling efforts and developed trade promotions for distributors. This is an example of a _____ strategy.
A. push
B. poke
C. pull
D. prospect
E. target

29. The Volvo name denotes safety while the Corvette brand brings images of speed and performance to many of the "Baby Boom" generation. In marketing, this is called
A. targeting.
B. segmenting.
C. positioning.
D. product penetration.
E. product development.

30. When Pepsi tried to enter the non-cola soft drink market using their existing brand to launch a new product, the result was Crystal Pepsi. Which market growth strategy was this?
A. market expansion
B. market development
C. market creation
D. product penetration
E. product development

CHAPTER FIVE
APPLICATIONS PROJECT

Purpose: To increase understanding of the marketing research process through the application of the five steps.

Instructions: Assume the role of Director of Admissions for your school. You are aware of decreasing freshman enrollment in your organization (a symptom). Hypothesize what the problem might be and suggest a plan for data collection. Remember to exhaust all secondary data opportunities before implementing primary data collection.

Step 1: Possible Research Hypothesis

Step 2: Developing a Research Plan

Step 3: Collect Data

    A. Sources of Secondary Data

        1. Internal

        2. External

    B. Primary Data Collection Method

        1. Observation

        2. Survey

            Mail

            Phone

            Personal

                Interviews

                Focus Groups

CHAPTER FIVE
EXAM PRACTICE QUESTIONS

The following questions are designed to test your comprehension of marketing concepts and terminology.

1. The two primary goals of marketing research are to
A. challenge the competition and win.
B. survey consumers and target specific markets.
C. improve the marketing mix and reduce uncertainty.
D. collect data and distribute it.
E. analyze consumers and attribute marketing.

2. The outcome of the problem identification stage of the research process is usually
A. a quantitative analysis.
B. coded results.
C. a set of hypotheses.
D. a research plan.
E. a data collection questionnaire.

3. A research plan should include
A. coding of data from responses.
B. interpretation of findings.
C. a summary of information found in secondary sources.
D. methodology, budget, and schedule for the research.
E. raw data from the questionnaire.

4. Taking a "backward approach" to research design means that planners design a research methodology starting with
A. goals, decisions, and actions.
B. budget and schedule.
C. a set of hypotheses.
D. examination of past trends.
E. a plan.

5. Your book calls large, often computerized, collections of information
A. databases.
B. information warehouses.
C. data complications.
D. information collections.
E. primary data.

6. The principle purpose of the stage of marketing research in which findings are presented is to
A. analyze data.
B. clearly define the methodology to be used.
C. help managers use the information to make decisions.
D. better define the problem.
E. entertain company management.

7. A total group of people about whom marketers wish to know something is called a
A. population.
B. sample.
C. survey.
D. focus group.
E. market segment.

8. A form of field experimentation in which a new product/strategy is given an initial trial in one or two selected market sites is called
A. survey research.
B. secondary collection.
C. test marketing.
D. scanning.
E. tracking study.

9. Which of the following does **NOT** describe focus group research?
A. the group should be representative of the population
B. it must be led by a trained moderator
C. must be limited to only one session to avoid bias
D. useful in exploratory research
E. gives marketers a better understanding of how the product is used or perceived

10. The great advantage of the observational method of data collection is its
A. ease of administration.
B. realistic reports on actual behavior.
C. ability to ask in-depth questions.
D. speed of retrieval.
E. explanation of why behavior occurred.

11. Zip code information and the U.S. census are considered
A. primary data.
B. random sampling.
C. test marketing.
D. secondary data.
E. qualitative research.

12. Quantitative research
A. employs some form of statistical analysis.
B. typically uses open-ended data collection methods.
C. provides insight into consumer motives.
D. is more interpretive than qualitative research.
E. is only used in exploratory research.

13. The most difficult step in the research process, according to your text, is
A. presenting findings.
B. coding the data.
C. collecting the data.
D. analyzing the data.
E. defining the problem.

14. Information is
A. the same as data.
B. raw material.
C. facts, statistics, and observations.
D. knowledge critical to planning and decision making
E. collected during step three of the research process.

15. Which of the following is NOT an accurate description of a marketing information system?
A. integrated, company-wide
B. processes internal and external data
C. assists in marketing decision making
D. manipulates databases to provide information
E. none, all describe a MIS

The remaining questions are designed evaluate your ability to apply the text concepts.
16. Pillsbury introduced Oven Lovin' cookie dough without knowing that consumers would not be willing to pay more for new packaging, but less volume. This failure is probably due to
A. poor portfolio analysis.
B. faulty management research.
C. insufficient marketing research.
D. insufficient product testing.
E. consumer denial.

17. After discovering some problems, Tombstone Pizza set up a process of monitoring discounting and pricing of all pizza sales to the trade and keeping detailed records of sales by product variety. This process is an example of a
A. marketing information system.
B. marketing research schemata.
C. sales tracking objective.
D. multiple information program.
E. media monitoring plan.

18. If XYZ Company wants to do research to further identify the true nature of the problem leading to a shortfall in sales in the previous year, they should probably undertake
A. a survey.
B. exploratory research.
C. experimental research.
D. quantitative research.
E. a direct mail study.
19. Smith Peanut Company is attempting to learn more about the positioning of their peanuts in consumers' minds. The company has interviewed 1 million consumers, and has found that their product is perceived by 80% of those interviewed as having fuller roasted taste, but that the peanuts are not salty enough. To be sure the findings are correct, the company is planning to interview another 500,000 consumers. Clearly the company is suffering from
A. marketing myopia.
B. improper problem definition.
C. insufficient data.
D. diversification risk analysis.
E. analysis paralysis.

20. Jim knows that he wants to be able to recommend a specific ad (from among several options) and an advertising schedule for that ad as a result of his research. He is designing his questions, his research methodology and his budget based on what he feels it will take to reach these decisions. Jim is using a
A. set of hypotheses.
B. backward approach.
C. trend analysis method.
D. quantitative method.
E. tracking study.

21. In order to predict her chances for election to the student government, Jane hired a friend to take a poll of students eating in the cafeteria and give her the results, without sharing them with any of her competitors. Jane hired her friend to collect:
A. secondary data.
B. indirect data.
C. experimental data.
D. primary data.
E. syndicated data.

22. Millennium hired the Clarion Research Company to collect data regarding the demographics of rechargeable battery users, their attitudes and level of satisfaction with Millennium and its competitors. Clarion produced a report which was for the exclusive use of Millennium. Results from this research would be
A. a syndicated study.
B. secondary data.
C. a marketing information system.
D. a tracking study.
E. primary data.

23. If Millennium obtained a numbered list of people in a certain community, put number tiles representing each of the numbers in a box and drew from the box, they would be selecting a
A. stratified sample.
B. convenience sample.
C. quota sample.
D. number-oriented sample.
E. random sample.

24. Eric runs a local camera shop. He keeps accurate records of sales, store traffic, customer's names and addresses, and inventory turnover. These facts would be
A. data.
B. information.
C. primary research.
D. test marketing.
E. sampling.

25. The owner of a local coffee shop makes it a habit to talk with each customer. She informally asks them about product quality and service satisfaction. This would be considered
A. environmental scanning.
B. secondary data.
C. random probability sampling.
D. test marketing.
E. database management.

26. Amtrack sent researchers on board their trains armed with passenger questionnaires to try to find out why people take the train. The type of research they were conducting is called
A. an experiment.
B. a survey.
C. a focus group.
D. on-board interrogation.
E. observation.

27. Sean's dry-cleaning was experiencing decreasing sales. He decided to initiate marketing research. His first step should be
A. collect data by measuring sales.
B. implement test marketing.
C. conduct exploratory research to define the problem.
D. develop the research plan.
E. analyze the secondary data.

28. Ann decided to keep track of store traffic in 15 minute intervals, build a database of all existing customers, and collect data on average length of stay in the store. This is _____ research.
A. qualitative
B. secondary
C. test marketing
D. quantitative
E. experimental

29. Which of the following would be best at providing qualitative research?
A. focus groups
B. test marketing
C. secondary data
D. database
E. mail survey

30. Ben's Bagels needed data on consumers in the neighborhood of his store. Because he had not taken any marketing courses in college, he was ignorant of sophisticated data collection methods. He decided to gather data by asking his customers where they lived and their service expectations. This would be considered an example of
A. secondary data.
B. primary data.
C. test marketing.
D. focus groups.
E. experimentation.

CHAPTER SIX
APPLICATIONS PROJECT

Purpose: To increase understanding of the "black box" model of consumer behavior.

Instructions: Using yourself as the proposed target market, analyze the external influences on your decision to go to your current college. Use text pages 201-213.

EXTERNAL INFLUENCES

Economic:

Geographic:

Culture:

Social:

Personal:

Instructions: Using the same target market as above, examine your decision making process. Use pages 219-222.

DECISION PROCESS

1. Problem recognition cues

2. Information Sources

    1.

    2.

    3.

    4.

3. Evaluation of Alternatives

     1.

     2.

     3.

     4.

4. Purchase

5. Post-purchase Evaluators

CHAPTER SIX
EXAM PRACTICE QUESTIONS

The following questions are designed to test your comprehension of marketing concepts and terminology.

1. The "black box" model of consumer behavior examines
A. the interaction of external and internal factors to produce behavior.
B. the use of a stimulus to elicit a patterned response from consumers.
C. how consumers attitudes toward an ad affect brand attitudes.
D. the feeling and behaviors of the African American subculture in the U.S..
E. the use of boxes to create certain behaviors by consumers.

2. Buying power is
A. the ability of a company to purchase sufficient media spots.
B. a company's ability to "buy" the consumers through advertising.
C. resources that people can exchange for goods or services.
D. the power of a consumer to influence decisions made by a manufacturer.
E. the ability of an advertiser to influence editorial content of media.

3. Any set of people whose outlook we use as a comparison for our own personal behavior is called a
A. modeling base.
B. peer group.
C. reference group.
D. comparable population.
E. comparison sample.

4. Cohort analysis examines
A. aspirational reference groups.
B. consumption behavior of couples.
C. groups of people who are close in age.
D. attitudes of buyers of a particular product.
E. how people organize themselves.

5. Relatively enduring feelings of favorableness or unfavorableness toward an object, an idea, or a behavior, are called
A. needs.
B. involvements.
C. motivations.
D. values.
E. attitudes.

6. Brand loyalty is most closely associated with the concept of
A. personality.
B. culture.
C. cognitive dissonance.
D. lifestyle.
E. attitude.

7. An uncomfortable state of mind in which a consumer experiences conflict between some belief, attitude, or value and a particular action, often characterized by buyer remorse, is called
A. tentative decision making.
B. purchase denial.
C. classical conditioning.
D. evoked behavior.
E. cognitive dissonance.

8. A broad influence on consumer behavior that describes a way of living is called
A. culture.
B. attitude.
C. census.
D. purchasing power.
E. market share.

9. Which of the following is **NOT** a type of reference group?
A. membership
B. aspirational
C. dissociative
D. culture
E. none, all of the above are types of reference groups

10. Advertisers use the activities, interests, and opinions that guide your way of living to communicate their message to a demographically diverse audience. This is called
A. lifestyle.
B. attitude.
C. reference groups.
D. cognitive dissonance.
E. black box.

11. Consumer behavior refers to the "black box" when trying to understand
A. external buying influences.
B. marketing mix variables.
C. level of consumer involvement.
D. the hidden mind of the consumer.
E. economic impact.

12. Maslow's hierarchy of needs attempts to explain
A. cognitive dissonance.
B. motivation.
C. learning.
D. attitude.
E. perception.
13. Attitudes are
A. relatively enduring feelings toward something.
B. a part of operant conditioning.
C. theories of motivation.
D. short term learning mechanisms.
E. temporary perceptual distortions.

14. The decisions that generate the maximum perceived risk are most likely to use
A. routine response solving.
B. limited problem solving.
C. cognitive information search.
D. extensive problem solving.
E. classical deductive search.

15. The alternatives considered in the decision-making process comprise the
A. early adopters.
B. inept set.
C. needs hierarchy.
D. information search.
E. evoked set.

The remaining questions are designed to evaluate your ability to apply the text concepts.

16. While it may be appropriate to use a hard-driving woman in an ad in the United States, this would probably not be appropriate in China. This difference in appropriateness stems primarily from a difference in
A. economic environments.
B. geographic orientation.
C. marketing mix strategies.
D. cultural values.
E. population characteristics.

17. In India, aspiration strategies are not used much in advertising because opportunity is based primarily on birth and there is little an individual can do to change this. This is an example of the importance of _____ in some cultures.
A. dissociative reference groups
B. social class structure
C. economic orientations
D. lineage consumption
E. cultural mavens

18. Millennium found that use of rechargeable batteries is greatest among families with children. This is an example of the effect of _____ on consumption patterns.
A. childhood orientation
B. social class structure
C. cultural values
 D. family life cycle
E. aspirational groups

19. One would expect reference groups to have the strongest influence on an individual who is purchasing
A. roses.
B. a car.
C. face cream.
D. a calculator.
E. a refrigerator.

20. When Eric went out to buy a computer he saw advertised on sale the week before, he found the sale price at the store to be higher than what he thought he remembered from the ad. The salesman showed him the ad to confirm that the current price was, in fact, the sale price which Eric saw. Eric probably had experienced some
A. classical conditioning.
B. information repositioning.
C. selective distortion.
D. price modeling.
E. price repositioning.

21. Children and animals are often used in advertising for which they do not have any particular relevance. Their use is probably intended to create "warm, fuzzy feelings" for the product through
A. classical conditioning.
B. operant conditioning.
C. creative learning.
D. selective perception.
E. cognitive dissonance.

22. Dan has just purchased a new suit for job interviewing. When he put the suit on, he realized his Reeboks and Docksiders were not going to be appropriate to wear with it and that he would need to buy a new pair of shoes. Dan is experiencing which step in the consumer decision making process?
A. information search
B. evaluation of alternatives
C. purchase
D. postpurchase satisfaction
E. problem recognition

23. Which of the following products would be most likely to involve extensive problem solving and a high level of information search by purchasers?
A. a bookbag
B. a computer
C. a belt
D. a six-pack of beer
E. a textbook

24. Every time his mother shopped the cereal aisle at the grocery store, Marvin would throw a tantrum until she bought his favorite cereal. Marvin was fulfilling a(n) _____ in the buying process.
A. attitude
B. role
C. reference
D. niche
E. external influence

25. Tom was worried about the opinions of his co-workers when he decided to shave his head. They were serving as a(n)
A. cultural value base.
B. membership reference group.
C. attitude determinant.
D. marketing niche.
E. dissociative refence group.

26. Chanel has just entered law school and wants to be a member of the law review at her school by her junior year. The law review members are a(n) _____ to Chanel.
A. dissociative reference group
B. associative reference group
C. aspirational reference group
D. membership reference group
E. inspirational reference group

27. The social chairman of Rob's fraternity is a trendsetter and widely admired by all the brothers. He would be considered a(n)
A. inspirator.
B. market nicher.
C. consumer advocate.
D. laggard.
E. opinion leader.

28. Steve loved sailing and was eagerly engulfed by all television programs and magazine articles on the subject. His single-mindedness for sailing caused him to "ignore" other things in his environment. This is called
A. selective perception.
B. selective attitude.
C. cognitive dissonance.
D. hierarchy of needs.
E. sensory level of involvement.

29. According to Maslow, a teenager who "hangs out" at the local sandwich shop because all his peers do the same is most likely responding to a need for
A. self esteem.
B. safety.
C. food.
D. belongingness.
E. spirituality.

30. When cramming for exams, Kim gets an uncontrollable craving for Ben & Jerry's Rainforest Crunch ice cream. If the local 24 hour store is out, she drives to wherever necessary to find the ice cream. Kim's behavior would be best described as
A. self actualizing.
B. cognitive dissonance.
C. brand loyal.
D. evoked set.
E. operant perception.

CHAPTER SEVEN
APPLICATIONS PROJECT

Purpose: To increase understanding of how organizational buying behavior differs from consumer buying behavior by analyzing the key factors in the business-to-business buying model.

Instructions: Discuss the differences in external factors and the buying organization if you were buying Harley-Davidson motorcycles for the local police department instead of personal use. Refer to Figure 7-2 and the Harley-Davidson case in the back of your book for additional insight.

External Factors
Buying situation: (Straight repurchase, modified repurchase, new purchase)

Branding:

Marketing communication:

Product specifications:

Buying Organization
Organizational influences:

Buying Center:

Personal/Interpersonal influence:

CHAPTER SEVEN
EXAM PRACTICE QUESTIONS

The following questions are designed to test your comprehension of marketing concepts and terminology.

1. Derived demand
A. demand for organizational goods which comes from consumer demand for products.
B. demand which is derived from foreign sources.
C. demand which is derived from organizational demand for raw materials.
D. demand which comes after sale.
E. demand which is based on the careful derivation of price ratios.

2. The three primary types of organizational markets are
A. government, education, and institutional.
B. retailing, wholesaling, and manufacturing.
C. raw materials, supplies, and services.
D. consumer, business, and government.
E. industrial, reseller, and government/institutional.

3. The industrial market is most likely to include
A. retailers.
B. government.
C. manufactures.
D. wholesalers.
E. hospitals.

4. The primary purpose of the Standard Industrial Classification (SIC) system is to
A. classify types of wholesalers.
B. classify approaches to industrial management.
C. create standard terminology and practices for total quality management systems.
D. categorize standard operations management procedures.
E. categorize firms according to the types of products they produce.

5. Companies which provide temporary workers for offices and other parts of business and industry are functioning primarily as
A. institutions.
B. consumers.
C. resellers.
D. modified repurchases.
E. industrial organizations.

6. In Japan, companies often develop strong corporate relationships in which companies buy each other's shares and agree to buy from each other. These groups are called
A. shimugis.
B. wallabangs.
C. partnersans.
D. keiretsus.
E. origatos.

7. The most important means of marketing communication in most organizational selling situations is
A. advertising.
B. marketing public relations.
C. packaging.
D. sales promotion.
E. personal selling.

8. What is the final step in the organizational buying process?
A. purchase
B. evaluation of alternatives
C. negotiation
D. information search
E. postpurchase evaluation

9. When compared to consumer purchasing, organizational purchase decisions
A. are more impacted by television advertising.
B. are usually made more quickly.
C. involve fewer people.
D. are more rational.
E. involve smaller product quantities.

10. Resellers measure the success of their purchasing decision based on
A. their customer's satisfaction.
B. the product's durability.
C. the number of product modifications necessary.
D. service provisions.
E. the parts compatibility with the final product.

11. The business-to-business, or organization, market is
A. about 1/3 the size of the consumer market.
B. about 1/4 the size of the consumer market.
C. about 10% of the size of the consumer market.
D. almost three times the size of the consumer market.
E. ten times the size of the consumer market.

12. A florist that buys from a farmer to sell to a hotel is part of the
A. organizational market.
B. consumer market.
C. government market.
D. end-user market.
E. non profit market.

13. Creating and maintaining customer satisfaction is
A. less important in organization markets than in consumer markets.
B. only an issue in consumer markets.
C. only an issue in organization markets.
D. more important in organization markets than in consumer markets.
E. only possible in consumer markets due to measurement constraints.

14. Organization buyers
A. buy in smaller volume than consumers.
B. depend less on long-term relationships.
C. rely heavily on advertising for information.
D. utilize relationship marketing.
E. are less structured than consumers in the buying process.

15. If Connie's catering automatically buys plates and napkins from the same suppliers whenever she needs to restock, she is engaging in a(n)
A. modified repurchase.
B. straight repurchase.
C. negotiation.
D. open bid.
E. new purchase.

The remaining questions are designed to evaluate your ability to apply the text concepts.

16. Millennium's rechargeable battery technology, called Intellilink, is sold to manufacturers of cellular telephones and other products. If consumers start buying fewer cellular telephones, then there will be less demand by manufacturers for Millennium battery units. This is an example of
A. technological reclassification.
B. distribution demand.
C. trade multiplier effect.
D. derived demand.
E. technology reorientation.

17. A seller of aluminum ore who needs the names of all aluminum fabricators who might want to buy his product within a given area would most likely use
A. a portfolio analysis.
B. a SWOT report.
C. a derived demand report.
D. an SIC report.
E. a regiocentric report.

18. Which of the following is most likely to be included in the government/institutional market?
A. Michelin tire company
B. Bloomingdale's department store
C. Steve's temporary employment service
D. Pace University
E. Cookies by Carolyn

19. If XYZ corporation decides it is unhappy with its current phone system and wants to purchase one that is more up-to-date on a number of different features, the company will most likely use
A. a purchasing allocation.
B. a new purchase.
C. an internal transaction.
D. a modified repurchase.
E. a straight repurchase.

20. When Ciba-Geigy developed a new anti-malarial drug for sale in the third world countries, it most likely focused primarily on _____ as the best form of marketing communications to reach physicians and hospitals.
A. advertising
B. marketing public relations
C. sales promotion
D. packaging
E. personal selling

21. Silicon chips that go into personal computers and lasers that read compact discs would be classified as
A. components.
B. consumer products.
C. raw materials.
D. filaments.
E. exponents.

22. In his job as the purchasing agent for a small company, Tom is responsible for dealing with all sales representatives trying to sell products to the company. He makes sure that the sales reps deal only with him and don't bother other people involved in the decision process. In this role, Tom is functioning as a
A. product manager.
B. communication orienter.
C. information manager.
D. company representative.
E. gatekeeper.

23. The purchase of a fire sprinkler system will require input from a variety of people. The accountants are concerned about its cost and the engineers are concerned about its design. Maintenance people are concerned about whether the installation will be messy. Workers are concerned about efficiency. Representatives of these groups can be collectively referred to as the organization's
A. purchasing department.
B. buying union.
C. decision makers.
D. buying center.
E. new task buying committee.

24. The local water company received input from the office staff before purchasing a copier. As described, the staff's role was
A. gatekeepers.
B. influencers.
C. a buying centers.
D. consumers.
E. derivers.

25. A purchasing manager asks manufacturers to supply brochures and other written information about their products, and with that information in hand, buying center members discuss how best to satisfy the company's needs with available products. This is the _____ stage in the organization buying process.
A. problem recognition
B. symptom survey
C. search for information
D. postpurchase
E. exploratory

26. According to the text criteria, which of the following ads for tires would be best for organization markets?
A. Michelin's emotional appeal for safety using a baby in a tire.
B. an Al Unser, Jr. testimonial on tire performance
C. a rational list of tire specifications and explanation of models
D. a humorous ad showing toddlers using a tire as a swing
E. a "sale" ad promoting free installation and balance

27. In the government market, which of the following products is most likely to be purchased through negotiated purchasing?
A. copier paper
B. office furniture
C. fire extinguishers
D. hospital sheets
E. nuclear reactors

28. Connie's Catering buys produce, meats, and pastry. The banquets she creates with these raw materials are then sold to other companies. Connie's Catering is part of the
A. industrial market.
B. consumer market.
C. government market.
D. institutional market.
E. reseller market.

29. Which of the following would be considered part of the reseller market?
A. JC Penney department store
B. General Motors Saturn manufacturing plant
C. Shands Teaching Hospital
D. US Army
E. all of the above

30. The school snack bar buys candy products from Hersey, soft drinks from Coca-Cola, and salty snacks from Frito Lay to sell to students. The snack bar is functioning primarily as part of the
A. non profit market.
B. government market.
C. reseller market.
D. industrial market.
E. consumer market

CHAPTER EIGHT
APPLICATIONS PROJECT

Purpose: To increase understanding of the micromarketing concept and provide an opportunity to apply the major criteria for segmenting a market.

Instructions: Read the box on pg. 255 in your text. Consider yourself a micromarket in the mass market of prospective students for your university. Describe your "micromarket" according to the market segmentation criteria listed.

Demographic Segmentation:
    Age/Life Stage:

    Gender:

    Ethnicity Religion:

    Income:

Geographic:
    International mobility:

    Preferred climate:

Psychographics:
    VALS 2 category:

Behavior:
    Usage rates:

    User status:

    Benefits sought:

Instructions: Discuss whether or not you feel it would be beneficial for your school to use a micromarketing strategy to attract students.

Instructions: Of the criteria listed in Part one, put an asterisk to the left of those important to all college recruiters. Remember, market segmentation is only effective if it is useful in predicting buying behavior. Which target market strategy would you recommend to your college? (undifferentiated, differentiated, concentrated) Why?

The following questions are designed to test your comprehension of marketing concepts and terminology.

1. Using the same marketing mix to sell to everyone is known as
A. differentiated marketing.
B. targeting.
C. segmenting.
D. mass marketing.
E. niche marketing.

2. Evaluating various segments and selecting the one that promises the best return on the firm's marketing investment is
A. differentiated marketing.
B. targeting.
C. segmenting.
D. mass marketing.
E. niche marketing.

3. Segmenting and targeting are very important in a marketing program because
A. the world is becoming more of a global village.
B. prospective customers really have the same basic needs.
C. marketers can match specific needs with specific marketing mixes.
D. all components of a product or service must be considered.
E. a message today needs to be very creative.

4. The most important factor in identifying market segments is to determine
A. shared demographic characteristics.
B. similar lifestyles.
C. a common language.
D. common needs.
E. similar ethnic backgrounds.

5. The VALS 2, Values and Lifestyles classification system uses _____ segmentation.
A. demographic
B. geographic
C. psychographic
D. popugraphic
E. behavior

6. If a firm uses mass marketing, then that firm is **NOT** using
A. undifferentiated marketing.
B. economies of scale.
C. market segmentation.
D. production efficiencies.
E. a single marketing mix.

7. Time series analysis relies on _____ to suggest what consumers will do.
A. historical purchasing behavior
B. concept testing
C. demand curve analysis
D. surveys
E. carefully defined future time periods

8. Segmentation
A. provides the basis for targeting.
B. provides the basis for mass marketing.
C. is only used in concentrated strategies.
D. is expected after targeting.
E. replaces the need for forecasting.

9. Age, occupation, and gender are
A. part of geographic segmentation.
B. part of demographic segmentation.
C. the only variables necessary for segmentation.
D. psychographic variables.
E. the best indicators of market demand.

10. The marketing strategy that is the most efficient utilization of limited resources is
A. shot gunning.
B. undifferentiated.
C. differentiated.
D. mass marketing.
E. concentrated marketing.

11. Micromarketing is
A. being all things to all people.
B. focusing on smaller segments of the population.
C. abstract and impersonal.
D. an abandoned and outdated marketing practice.
E. similar to mass marketing.

12. Forecasting
A. is the estimation of future events.
B. can use hard data analysis.
C. can use judgment or intuition.
D. is described by all of the above.
E. A and B only.

13. Trying to pinpoint the amount of product a company expects to sell during a specific time with a specified level of marketing and a specific marketing mix is the job of a
A. market forecast.
B. sales forecast.
C. market potential.
D. sales potential.
E. market demand device.

14. A market targeted by a company because of its "fit," even though the markets size is relatively small is called a
A. thimble.
B. microcosm.
C. niche.
D. mass market.
E. differentiated market.

15. Carnival Cruise Lines promotes to the couples market with television, to the family market segment using direct mail, and to the senior citizen segment through magazine advertising. Which targeting strategy is Carnival using?
A. concentrated marketing
B. mass marketing
C. undifferentiated marketing
D. differentiated marketing
E. niche marketing

The remaining questions are designed to evaluate your ability to apply the text concepts.

16. There are many different groups within the population that have differing needs for soft drinks, i.e. the dieters, the caffeine-avoiders, the sugar lovers, the wake-me-uppers, etc. When soft drink companies identify these groups, they are practicing
A. undifferentiated marketing.
B. targeting.
C. segmention.
D. mass marketing.
E. niche marketing.

17. The fact that producers have to modify electrical products for global markets to ensure that they will work on differing local electrical systems in different countries illustrates the need for _____ segmentation.
A. popugraphic
B. psychographic
C. behavior
D. geographic
E. electrical

18. Dockers pants were developed for the changing physiques of baby boomer males who still pursue an active life. The pants are wider in the seat than those typically worn by teenage males. The market for Dockers was segmented using
A. behavior characteristics and popugraphics.
B. psychographics and geographics.
C. demographics and psychographics.
D. psychographics and behavioral characteristics.
E. benefits sought and popugraphic.

19. Chicago's Old Town district has a heavy concentration of singles. The Sears store located there features hardware, home improvements, and ready-to-assemble furniture. The Sears store on Chicago's South Side features products for children because the neighborhood is composed of young families. This is an example of a response to segmenting using
A. geodemographics.
B. regionalization.
C. geographic specialization.
D. psychogeographics.
E. market delineation.

20. If Anheuser-Busch selects heavy beer drinkers as a target segment for its basic Budweiser beer, it is segmenting using
A. user status.
B. buyer orientation.
C. consumer orientation
D. usage rates.
E. benefits sought.

21. If Mystic Mint Cookies selected as a target segment people who want to have fresh breath, the company would be using a _____ segmentation.
A. demographic
B. geographic
C. oral
D. benefit
E. behavior

22. The Bank of Asia's development and marketing of MyCard for women in Hong Kong is an example of
A. undifferentiated marketing.
B. targeting.
C. segmenting.
D. mass marketing.
E. micromarketing.

23. Shelly's Tall Women's catalogue, designed for women 5'7 and taller, is practicing which targeting strategy?
A. concentrated marketing
B. undifferentiated marketing
C. overall marketing
D. generic marketing
E. differentiated marketing

24. Parker is in charge of the concessions for the school carnival. To determine the quantity of food to order, he looks at the previous year's sales. Parker is engaging in
A. survey execution.
B. demand intensity analysis.
C. elasticity analysis.
D. time series analysis.
E. concept testing.

25. Trevor's Toy Town features Barney, the purple dinosaur adored by pre-schoolers, in his store window to attract children. This is an example of _____ segmentation.
A. geographic
B. psychographic
C. demographic
D. socioeconomic
E. consumption pattern

26. Zip code cluster segmentation is an example of
A. personality.
B. behavior.
C. VALS 2.
D. geodemographics.
E. socioeconomic.

27. Walt Disney World offers Florida residents a discounted admission during the Fall season slow months. During slow winter months, they advertise "package deals" to Midwest residents. This is using _____ segmentation.
A. psychoecographic
B. geographic
C. socioeconomic
D. user status
E. personality

28. Breyers has expanded their product mix to include a line of high quality, fancy desserts. They selected as a target market people who entertain a lot. They are using
A. demographic segmentation.
B. psychographic segmentation.
C. geographic segmentation.
D. socioeconomic segmentation.
E. mass marketing segmentation.

29. In the 90's, a popular market segment is the OPALS (older people with active lifestyles). This is _____ segmentation.
A. geographic
B. behavior
C. social class
D. psychographic
E. econoage

30. Pepsi AM was developed for people who drink cola first thing in the morning. Jolt colas was developed with more caffeine to help the students stay awake while studying. These are both segmentation examples using
A. geodemographic variables.
B. behavior variables.
C. social class variables
D. life stage variables.
E. demographic variables.

CHAPTER NINE
APPLICATIONS PROJECT

Purpose: To increase understanding of the concept and tools of positioning in marketing strategy.

Instructions: Positioning is the act of formulating a marketing mix that locates the product in the mind of the customer in relation to the offering of competitors. Using The Body Shop case in the back of your textbook and your own personal buying experiences, determine the relevant product attributes. Give a brief justification for each choice.

Attribute list:

1.

2.

3.

4.

5.

Instructions: From the list indicate the two **MOST** important attributes with a star. Then develop a two-dimensional perceptual map to show where customers locate The Body Shop and at least **5** of their competitors.

Instructions: Is positioning by attribute the appropriate positioning strategy for The Body Shop? Briefly explain or suggest alternative from those listed on pages 306-309.

CHAPTER NINE
EXAM PRACTICE QUESTIONS

The following questions are designed to test your comprehension of marketing concepts and terminology.

1. Competitive advantage results from the
A. organizational mission statement.
B. creation of value for customers.
C. creation of possession utility.
D. execution of marketing tactics.
E. implementation of organizational budgets.

2. Products whose features, performance, and quality are equal to those of competitors are called _____ products.
A. equality
B. comparable
C. evoked
D. premium
E. parity

3. Cost leadership, product differentiation, cost focus, and differentiation focus are generic business strategies outlined by Michael Porter for achieving
A. promotion power.
B. competitive advantage.
C. market leadership.
D. marketing myopia.
E. marketing expertise.

4. If a firm has a product differentiation advantage, it means that
A. it can offer the lowest price and most value to consumers.
B. it has carefully defined a narrow market and modified a product to meet its needs.
C. its products have an actual or perceived uniqueness in a broad market.
D. it has successfully repositioned the competition.
E. it has market leadership in a broad array of markets.

5. When a company allows other firms to introduce products and checks market response before changing or introducing its own products, it is known as
A. market leader.
B. market follower.
C. market challenger.
D. cost leader.
E. cost challenger.

6. The key to maintaining competitive advantage, according to William Deming, and your textbook, is
A. being committed to constant improvement.
B. always being a leader with all products.
C. coordinating all innovative efforts.
D. challenging all markets.
E. stressing low price advantages in all areas.

7. If a company stresses product features in its promotion it is using
A. communication by use.
B. positioning by use.
C. communication by attributes.
D. positioning by benefits.
E. marketing by objectives.

8. Perceptual maps are used primarily in
A. positioning strategy development.
B. product differentiation.
C. advertising campaigns.
D. marketing segmentation.
E. media schedules.

9. According to your text, which of the following is NOT included in an evaluation of competitive advantage?
A. competition's strengths
B. products weaknesses
C. consumers' wants
D. product strengths
E. competitions weaknesses

10. Which of the following business practices would most likely be used by a proactive market follower?
A. mass marketing
B. copy cat product development
C. risk avoidance
D. focus on refining the market leader's innovations
E. challenge the market leader directly

11. A reactive market follower
A. is the same as a proactive market follower but with a higher-priced product.
B. embodies TQM principles.
C. plays catch-up by copying a leader's innovations.
D. has a product differentiation strategy for creating competitive advantage.
E. holds twice the market share of their nearest competitor.

12. Positioning is
A. the act of formulating a marketing mix which places a product in the consumer's mind.
B. a feedback mechanism.
C. executed independent of competition.
D. developing new products internally.
E. assuring retail gives you adequate shelf space.

13. The marketing concept emphasizes customer satisfaction. The positioning strategy most closely based on this goal is positioning by
A. price.
B. use.
C. product benefit.
D. behavior.
E. geography.

14. A strategy of positioning based on a product's ability to fulfill many functions is positioning by
A. price.
B. use.
C. user.
D. benefits.
E. brand loyalty.

15. Cost leadership is a sustainable competitive advantage only if
A. the firm is a monopoly.
B. barriers exist that prevent competitors from achieving the same low costs.
C. your product is a convenience good.
D. you are also the market leader.
E. a concentrated market segmentation strategy is used.

The remaining questions are designed to evaluate your ability to apply the text concepts.

16. Arby's ran a marketing communications campaign that offers its roast beef sandwich as an alternative to all those guys who wanted you to eat hamburgers. The campaign included "candid" shots of Wendy's and Ronald McDonald sneaking into Arby's for a change of pace. Arby's was using a positioning campaign based on
A. brand loyalty.
B. quality.
C. feature.
D. product category.
E. competitors.

17. The Japanese have been able to offer some of the lowest priced products to consumers around the world, achieving a leadership position in many markets based primarily on
A. product differentiation advantage.
B. narrow focus advantage.
C. price production advantage.
D. price guarantee advantage.
E. cost leadership advantage.

18. Maytag's "lonely repairman" ad campaign which stressed the reliability of Maytag washing machines, has helped Maytag to achieve
A. a narrow-focus advantage.
B. a cost leadership advantage.
C. distribution leadership.
D. a product differentiation advantage.
E. marketing communications control.

19. Cray Research's decision to produce and sell only supercomputers, a relatively small $1.7 billion worldwide market, used mostly for scientific purposes, and to stay away from minicomputers, is an example of a _____ strategy.
A. product differentiation
B. target value
C. differentiation focus
D. market challenger
E. parity product

20. If Procter and Gamble hold a 40% share of the laundry detergent market in the U.S., while Colgate Palmolive holds 20% and other companies hold the remaining 40% among them, Procter and Gamble would be considered a
A. market leader.
B. market challenger.
C. market follower.
D. brand superstar.
E. brand dominator.

21. The Acura Legend, Lexus, and Infinity, sell for about half the price of a comparably sized Mercedes or BMW automobile in the U.S. These companies are pursuing _____ strategies.
A. diversification
B. price leadership
C. reactive following
D. market innovation
E. generic market

22. Snap on Tools has a competitive advantage over its competitors in the mechanics market because it sells its tools right off trucks which call on automotive garages around the United States. This firm is using a _____ strategy.
A. product leadership
B. cost leadership
C. market follower
D. distribution leadership
E. selective distribution

23. When Honda took advantage of Harley Davidson's focus on the large motorcycle segment by entering with small models and growing into the larger ones, it was an example of Honda's use of a _____ strategy.
A. collaboration
B. weakness crumbling
C. layers of advantage
D. loose bricks
E. positioning the competition

24. How could a day-care center that specializes in newborns best use a perceptual map?
A. to locate its customer base
B. to determine target market demographics
C. to evaluate the position of competitors
D. to evaluate possible market share
E. to decide on a price range

25. To Trident gum, Wrigley's Doublemint and Dentyne would be considered
A. indirect competition.
B. the evoked set.
C. positioning allies.
D. direct competition.
E. brand intruders.

26. When you go to the grocery store to satisfy a sweet tooth craving, Ben and Jerry's ice cream, Oreo cookies, and Enternman's brownies function as
A. product differentials.
B. perceptual selectives.
C. product mixes.
D. direct competitors.
E. indirect competitors.

27. Which of the following would most likely be part of Lipton bottled tea's indirect competition?
A. York Peppermint Patty
B. Cambell Cheddar Cheese Soup
C. Del Monte canned peaches
D. Bic's disposable razor
E. Sprite lemon-lime soda

28. As a new brand entry into the market, which of the following products is most likely to be described as a parity product?
A. athletic shoes
B. textbooks
C. paper clips
D. laundry soap
E. soft drink

29. When Apple introduced their PC, they positioned directly against the market leader IBM, using fun and ease-of-use as a relative advantage. In this example, Apple is a
A. market leader.
B. cost leader.
C. market follower.
D. flanker.
E. market challenger.

30. Rooms To Go is a furniture retailer. They locate their stores in high traffic shopping areas and guarantee three day delivery. Their competitive advantage is based on
A. distribution leadership.
B. mass marketing.
C. cost leadership.
D. market challenger.
E. communications leadership.

CHAPTER TEN
APPLICATIONS PROJECT

Purpose: To increase understanding of the different types of branding strategies and brand name criteria.

Instructions: List 5 corporate brands for each category.
Product:

Brand Extension:

1.

2.

3.

4.

5.

Tiered Branding:

1.

2.

3.

4.

5.

Instructions: Using Table 10-1, compare five of the brands listed above to the text criteria for what a brand name should be. How do they rate?

CHAPTER TEN
EXAM PRACTICE QUESTIONS

The following questions are designed to test your comprehension of marketing concepts and terminology.

1. "A complex bundle of images, promises and experiences in the customer's mind" is how your text defines
A. a product.
B. a brand.
C. a marketing mix.
D. an advertising campaign.
E. positioning.

2. A brand image is the sum of
A. characters used to signify a brand name.
B. graphics used to depict a product.
C. components that make up the product.
D. impressions that affect how we perceive a brand.
E. advertising messages conveyed for a brand.

3. Brand equity refers to
A. the amount of investment a company has in a brand.
B. the value attached to a brand due to the relationship built with consumers.
C. brands which have developed similar images with the same target groups.
D. return on investment received on any given brand in a defined period of time.
E. the number of brands which a company "owns".

4. When a single brand name is used to identify a family on product line, it is called
A. private branding.
B. generic branding.
C. tiered branding.
D. multiple branding.
E. brand extension.

5. To have a global brand means to
A. use different brand names in different countries.
B. sell a product in every country of the world.
C. give a product a cosmopolitan sounding name.
D. use the same brand name and positioning strategy worldwide.
E. create an image of a worldwide product.

6. When a consumer remembers having seen a brand, it is called
A. brand acceptance.
B. brand recognition.
C. brand rememberance.
D. alertness index.
E. brand image.

7. The 4 steps which your book says customers must go through before they are brand loyal are
A. awareness, acceptance, preference, and action.
B. awareness, decision, agreement, and repurchase.
C. acceptance, preference, decision, and conviction.
D. preference, action, conviction, and dissonance.
E. action, desire, dissonance, and fortitude.

8. The people who ultimately make the decision about a brand's value are
A. brand managers.
B. customers.
C. stockholders.
D. competitors.
E. none of the above.

9. A private label brand is also called a
A. generic brand.
B. manufacturer brand.
C. store brand.
D. off brand.
E. limited use brand.

10. Which of the following is FALSE when defining trademarks?
A. they must be legally registered
B. they are part of the brand image
C. they give exclusive rights to the holder
D. they are identical to logo
E. none of the above, all define a trademark

11. Franchising is a type of
A. brand management.
B. licensing.
C. product management.
D. trademark enforcement.
E. brand personality.

12. Branding is
A. in the mind of the consumer.
B. the sum of the product's attributes.
C. only an issue when stimulating primary demand.
D. the fifth "p" in the marketing mix.
E. a segmentation philosophy.

13. Procter & Gamble is most known for their _____ system of brand management which introduces a new brand name for each new product.
A. tiered branding
B. brand extension
C. private branding
D. multiple branding
E. franchising

14. Before a customer can be taught to be brand loyal, they must pass through the _____ steps of
A. brand dissonance
B. brand conviction
C. brand preference
D. brand equity
E. cognitive dissonance

15. Using a brand extension strategy is dangerous because
A. consumers could forget the brand name.
B. brand personalities may clash.
C. new product introductions assume existing brand image.
D. marketing costs are higher for new product introductions.
E. all of the above.

The remaining questions are designed to evaluate your ability to apply the text concepts.
16. In a study of cake mixes, women were asked to draw a woman who would use Duncan-Hines cake mixes. Respondents drew pictures of career women who juggled family and business. When the same respondents were asked to draw pictures of women who would use Betty Crocker mixes, they drew stereotypical housewives. Which of the following most directly affects the respondents' reactions to these two brands?
A. the evoked set of the respondents
B. the brand image of the two products
C. the similarity of the two products
D. attitudinal differences of respondents
E. the fact that the products compete in an oligopolistic marketplace

17. Eric always buys Tide to wash his clothes even though many of the other brands cost about $1.00 less per container. The extra that he is willing to pay to buy Tide would be called Tide's
A. brand equity.
B. brand integral.
C. price power.
D. price integral.
E. brand image.

18. A private brand is
A. usually advertised internationally.
B. manufacturer's most valuable asset.
C. sold exclusively by one retailer or distributor.
D. controlled by just one manufacturer.
E. another name for a generic brand.

19. When Kelloggs names its cereals with both its company name and product brand name (e.g., Kelloggs Product 19), it is using
A. private branding.
B. generic branding.
C. tiered branding.
D. multiple branding.
E. brand extension.

20. The Mars corporation used to sell Snickers candy bars in Great Britain under the name of Marathon and under other names in other markets. During the late 1980's, it switched to a more standardized strategy and now sells the candy bar under the name of Snickers in all markets. Mars switched from
A. a global brand to a world product.
B. a transnational product to a multiple brand.
C. a global brand to a transnational brand.
D. a world product to a global brand.
E. a transnational brand to a global brand.

21. Many Atlanta Braves fans find Tommy LaSorda, manager of the Los Angeles Dodgers, distasteful. Because he is the spokesperson for SlimFast, some of the Braves fans would not buy the product. Their refusal to buy SlimFast is referred to as
A. brand disclaimer.
B. brand nonrecognition.
C. brand rejection.
D. consumer repeal.
E. consumer dissension.

22. The local Apple computer dealer surveyed the local high school and found 95% of students were familiar with their product. This would mean brand _____ is 95% in that school.
A. acceptance
B. awareness
C. rejection
D. necessity
E. preference

23. The Pillsbury Dough Boy is friendly and is dressed to symbolize "home cooking." He is an example of
A. a brand personality.
B. a personality logo.
C. a trademark.
D. a brand equity.
E. a perceptual mark.

24. Allstate's "hands" and The Traveller's "umbrella", are each an example of the insurance companies'
A. logo.
B. brand personality.
C. trademark.
D. license.
E. brand equity.

25. According to the text criteria, branding is most important to which group of products?
A. specialty goods
B. parity goods
C. luxury services
D. generics
E. new, innovative goods

26. Lady Lee products are sold exclusively by Kash-n-Karry. They are an example of a
A. private brand.
B. generic brand.
C. manufacturer brand.
D. logo brand.
E. tiered brand.

27. Pepsi uses the same brand name around the world and employs basically the same marketing strategy. Pepsi is an example of a
A. world product.
B. cross-cultural brand.
C. private brand.
D. global brand.
E. tiered brand.

28. Mark told his classmates he had a miserable time on the new playground at the local Burger King. Now Mark and his classmates refuse to go to Burger King. This is an example of
A. brand loyalty.
B. brand preference.
C. brand rejection.
D. brand ignorance.
E. brand equity.

29. Rush Limbaugh's choice as spokesperson for Florida oranges has been controversial. Limbaugh supporters most likely would be brand _____ to Florida oranges in support of someone they admire.
A. rejected
B. differentiated
C. accepted
D. loyal
E. repellant

30. Jim always goes to Wendy's for lunch. Co-workers invite him to go to other places with them, but Jim declines in favor of Wendy's. Jim would be considered _____ to Wendy's.
A. brand dysfunctional
B. brand rejected
C. product oriented
D. cognitively consistent
E. brand loyal

CHAPTER ELEVEN
APPLICATIONS PROJECT

PART 1
Purpose: To increase understanding of the goods classification system.

Instructions: Goods classified according to buyer orientation may change categories as the buying situation changes. Give a brief description of the buyer who would be considered under each heading. Put an asterisk in the category that is the most common description of the good.

CONVENIENCE   PREFERENCE   SHOPPING   SPECIALTY

Tires

Blue Jeans

VCR

Bicycle

Highlighter

Baseball Cap

PART 2
Purpose: To utilize creativity and to apply brand extension knowledge.

Instructions: Choose four of the product above, list your favorite brand, then brainstorm a possible brand extension.

PRODUCT LINE   BRAND   BRAND EXTENSION

1.

2.

3.

4.

CHAPTER ELEVEN
EXAM PRACTICE QUESTIONS

The following questions are designed to test your comprehension of marketing concepts and terminology.

1. The physical attributes that are characteristics of products are called
A. product benefits.
B. positioning factors.
C. product features.
D. goods elements.
E. selling propositions.

2. Most consumers choose a product on the basis of what the product will do for them. This is referred to as
A. product features.
B. product benefits.
C. product elements.
D. positioning outcomes.
E. problem dissections.

3. The way a product is created, styled, or fashioned is called
A. product features.
B. product benefits.
C. product elements.
D. positioning image.
E. product design.

4. A warranty benefits buyers by
A. improving product performance.
B. extending the product life cycle.
C. reducing their risk.
D. providing a universal product code.
E. expanding the product mix.

5. A _____ assures the buyer that the product can be returned if the performance isn't satisfactory.
A. warranty
B. quality control
C. product promise
D. product life cycle
E. guarantee

6. Goods purchased frequently at a relatively low price and used up rapidly are called
A. durable goods.
B. white goods.
C. specialty goods.
D. disposables.
E. consumables.

7. In the maturity stage of the product life cycle, sales are _____ and profits are _____.
A. growing, high
B. low, high
C. growing, high
D. high, variable
E. low, variable

8. Traditional U.S. quality control programs focus on
A. economies of scale.
B. product differentiation.
C. defect testing.
D. innovation
E. controlling inventory.

9. According to your text, which of the following is NOT true of a warranty?
A. it is a formal statement
B. includes manufacturer's liability for replacement\repair
C. it is an intangible feature of goods
D. is unnecessary for durable goods
E. provides buyers with recourse

10. Usually marketed based on distinctive features and level of quality, _____ goods are expected to last for several years.
A. consumable
B. nondurable
C. durable
D. convenience
E. services

11. Goods which are inexpensive durables that have been re-manufactured to offer the additional convenience of throwaway use are
A. disposables.
B. white goods.
C. green goods.
D. collectables.
E. capital goods.

12. Convenience goods involve
A. high risk, low effort.
B. low risk, low effort.
C. high effort, high involvement.
D. high effort, low involvement.
E. high risk, high involvement.
13. The power of branding is the basic difference between
A. disposables and durables.
B. consumables and disposables.
C. convenience and preference products.
D. preference and specialty products.
E. capital and commodity items.

14. The collection of products and product lines available from a given manufacturer is
A. the product mix.
B. the product life cycle.
C. a UPS plan.
D. the product SKU.
E. the brand extension.

15. The product life cycle describes
A. the stages of product development.
B. the stages through which a product evolves in the marketplace.
C. product classification.
D. a product positioning hierarchy.
E. brand recognition.

The remaining questions are designed to evaluate your ability to apply the text concepts.

16. Timex makes watches for skiers with a thermometer, oversize control buttons, and a strap which fits over heavy skiwear. Timex is differentiating these watches primarily based on product _____.
A. features
B. classification
C. life cycle
D. attitude
E. fashion

17. The voltage and cycle requirements need to be adjusted for electrical appliances in some international markets. This is an example of a(n) _____ consideration.
A. product life cycle
B. attribution
C. quality control
D. product benefit
E. method of operation

18. At three points in the production process, assembly workers pull a sample of Nightingale mail boxes and examine the boxes for leakage, strength, and endurance. These examinations are
A. benchmarks.
B. marketing research.
C. quality-control checkpoints.
D. warranty compliance systems.
E. quality control programs.

19. The Target store chain has a policy of accepting any returned items, regardless of the reason, and tries to make its customers feel comfortable with the return process. Target is using its _____ to gain competitive advantage.
A. quality issuance
B. guarantee
C. customer control procedures
D. quality control manifest
E. product screening

20. The best example of a capital good is
A. a machine used to grind wheat into flour.
B. paper for the company facsimile machine.
C. toothpaste.
D. a refrigerator.
E. a business suit.

21. Tide, All, Cheer, Dash, and Gain are all detergents manufactured by Procter and Gamble. They are an example of a
A. product mix.
B. product line.
C. product segment.
D. market offering.
E. brand extension.

22. Colgate Palmolive produces a wide variety of products, ranging from Kick the Habit (a stop-smoking product) to Colgate toothpaste and Palmolive bar soap. This variety indicates extensive
A. depth of product line.
B. width of product mix.
C. width of product line.
D. depth of product mix.
E. extent of brand extension.

23. When a new product steals sales and market share away from the same company's existing products, it is called
A. product extension.
B. product life cycle.
C. cannibalization.
D. share disturbance.
E. brand theft.

24. Four wheel drive, air conditioning and a CD player stereo system would be considered
A. product benefits.
B. product features.
C. product life cycles.
D. product positioning.
E. classification criteria.

25. J. Crew advertises wool socks to hikers because they help keep feet drier and warmer. This is positioning based on product
A. attributes.
B. features.
C. price.
D. benefits.
E. design.

26. When Honda was sued by ATV owners for injuries from careless safety design, it was an example of _____ issue.
A. product differentiation
B. product benefits
C. safety council standards
D. product positioning
E. product liability

27. The best example of a good which would probably be classified as a consumable is
A. a refrigerator.
B. a rare coin.
C. snow skis.
D. a loaf of bread.
E. a toaster.

28. The concern a student experiences when choosing a college regarding that school's ability to prepare them for the job market would be called
A. preference.
B. risk.
C. frequency.
D. effort.
E. timing.

29. Level of involvement is greatest when buying
A. specialty goods.
B. convenience goods.
C. expense goods.
D. durable goods.
E. disposables.

30. The best example of a shopping good would be
A. chewing gum.
B. a candy bar.
C. a box of cereal.
D. a bottle of mouthwash.
E. a pair of jeans.

CHAPTER TWELVE
APPLICATIONS PROJECT

Purpose: To expand knowledge and increase understanding of the challenge of marketing service product.

Instructions: Discuss each of the characteristics of service products as they pertain to the Southwest Airlines case on pages 400-401 in your textbook.

Intangibility:

Close Customer Relationship:

Perishability:

Product Inseparable from Producer:

Quality Variability:

Instructions: Discuss the "service attitude" of Southwest.

CHAPTER TWELVE
EXAM PRACTICE QUESTIONS

The following questions are designed to test your comprehension of marketing concepts and terminology.

1. A company's location on the goods-services continuum relates to its
A. degree of goods provided vs. services provided.
B. depth of product line.
C. number of brand extensions in the service area.
D. guarantee policies.
E. type of physical features provided.

2. Companies who sell primarily services, rather than goods, are referred to collectively as
A. service manufacturers.
B. ancillary manufacturers.
C. the third sector.
D. secondary manufacturers.
E. the service sector.

3. A "service product" is defined as
A. a product which is secondary to the principal being sold.
B. a task or action whose performance by a seller offers some benefit.
C. that which accompanies the sale of a product.
D. a product of a non-profit company.
E. consultation for a company or customer.

4. The customer relationship characteristic of services described in your text means that
A. the service is depended on the performance of a task.
B. quality is variable.
C. customers' needs are more homogeneous.
D. economies of scale are difficult to achieve.
E. the cooperation of the customer is needed.

5. The service characteristic of perishability described in your text means that
A. the service is dependent on the performance of the risk.
B. customers' needs are more homogeneous.
C. quality is variable.
D. a service is not something one can touch.
E. if the service is not utilized to capacity, it cannot be stored for later use.

6. Identifying and measuring factors that affect customer satisfaction in service industries is called
A. benchmarking.
B. factorial analysis.
C. issue measurement.
D. service identification.
E. problem classification.

7. "Mystery shoppers" often help service businesses with
A. employee training programs.
B. customer satisfaction surveys.
C. capacity management programs.
D. performance evaluation programs.
E. marketing analysis.

8. According to your text, the most important aspect of distribution in the service industry is
A. channel length.
B. convenience to the customer.
C. markup requirements.
D. wholesale networks.
E. dealer experience.

9. Which of the following is NOT one of the major characteristics of services?
A. perishability
B. variability in quality
C. inseparability from provider
D. consistency
E. intangibility

10. Coordinating supply and demand is crucial to services. This process is called
A. resource sourcing.
B. capacity management.
C. salary maximization.
D. resource bungling.
E. economic management.

11. Services tend to be labor intensive, this is mostly clearly exhibited in their characteristic of
A. perishability.
B. quality.
C. consistency.
D. variability.
E. inseparability.

12. Successful companies emphasize employee training to overcome the service characteristic of
A. benchmarking.
B. tangibility.
C. perishability.
D. reciprocity.
E. variability in quality.

13. U.S. consumer spend
A. more on durable goods than on services.
B. less on durable goods than on services.
C. the same on durable goods and services.
D. 90% of disposable income on services.
E. less on services than other cultures.

14. Internationally, services
A. are not exportable.
B. are decreasing in rate of growth.
C. are one of the fastest growing business sectors.
D. are too deeply rooted in national culture to expand into non domestic markets.
E. are more universal in quality.

15. Services marketing differs from goods marketing in that
A. a target market is unnecessary.
B. services often combine product and distribution.
C. employees are less important to services marketing programs.
D. distribution channels are usually longer for service firms.
E. quality is not a consideration for services.

The remaining questions are designed to evaluate your ability to apply the text concepts.
16. When fertilizer firms offer to contract to apply fertilizer for their customers, it is an example of what your text calls
A. aftermarketing.
B. added promotion.
C. service extension.
D. missionary selling.
E. contractual marketing.

17. One insurance company commercial shows a younger mother and child having to leave their beautiful home because dad dies without enough insurance, dramatizing the benefits of the service. This dramatization is important because of the _____ characteristic of services.
A. inseparability
B. customer relations
C. perishability
D. intangibility
E. variability in quality

18. After the Friday high school football games, the local McDonald's restaurant doubles the number of people it usually has working in order to feed the people who want something to eat after the game. This scheduling strategy is called
A. relationship marketing.
B. service balancing.
C. supply balancing.
D. capacity management.
E. marketing mixing.

19. Every time Wendy goes to the clinic for her allergy shots, she is treated by a different nurse. She evaluates the clinic's service based on her experiences. This is due to the _____ characteristic of services.
A. inseparability
B. customer relations
C. intangibility
D. perishability
E. variability in quality

20. At Southwest Airlines, employees are encouraged to have fun and make flying an enjoyable experience for themselves and for the customers. This approach reflects
A. tangibility.
B. service attitude.
C. perishability.
D. capacity management.
E. pricing strategy.

21. To help employees understand older customers, one Pennsylvania bank asks employees to fill out deposit slips with Vaseline smeared on their glasses and to count money with fingers taped together. This is part of the company's
A. employee training program.
B. benchmarking program.
C. capacity management program.
D. performance evaluation program.
E. marketing analysis.

22. Dentists often have one rate for cavity filling, one rate for teeth cleaning, one rate for root canals, etc. This system of pricing is called
A. set fee.
B. periodic change.
C. activity fee.
D. fixed base.
E. commission.

23. Which of the following is the best example of "the service sector"?
A. a candy bar manufacturer
B. a drycleaner
C. a motorcycle producer
D. a greeting card company
E. a ski manufacturer

24. Which of the following is LEAST likely to be considered a service?
A. The Gap Specialty retail
B. Nordstrom's department stores
C. Maytag Appliance Manufacturer
D. Fantastic Sam's haircutters
E. First Union bank

25. Extra activities by Oil Can Henry's such as free car a wash, complementary newspaper and coffee, and a flower for women customers, are designed to enhance the sale are referred to as
A. facilitating services.
B. product services.
C. substitute services.
D. service extensions.
E. brand extension

26. Allstate's "good hands" logo is an attempt to convey security to customers. This is an example of a strategy to deal with the _____ characteristic of services.
A. variability
B. inseparability
C. perishability
D. constancy
E. intangibility

27. Many restaurants offer early bird specials and happy hour deals to overcome the _____ characteristic of services.
A. intangibility
B. perishability
C. tangibility
D. spontaneity
E. customer relations.

28. The local university wanted to improve their turnaround time for a financial aid reply. They measured 10 other area school's to determine an industry average. This was an example of a _____ activity.
A. illegal search
B. service classification
C. benchmarking
D. capacity management
E. aftermarketing

29. Many large advertising agencies charge their customers a fee based on a percentage of total media cost, this is called _____ pricing.
A. set fee
B. sliding scale
C. salary
D. commission
E. capacity rebate

30. Ben went to breakfast at Denny's and encountered a rude waitperson who never refilled his coffee mug and delivered cold food. Ben now discourages everyone from eating at Denny's. This is a common problem for service businesses resulting from the universal service characteristic of
A. perishability.
B. intangibility.
C. consistency.
D. customer indifference.
E. inseparability.

CHAPTER THIRTEEN
APPLICATIONS PROJECT

Purpose: To increase familiarity with the first two steps of the new product development process.

Instructions: Choose an existing branded product from which to develop a new product idea. Explain your "new" product in Step 1 and classify it as a product innovation, improvement, or invention.

Current Brand:

Step #1...Idea Generation:

Instructions: Screen your idea according to Table 13-3.

Step #2...Screening:

Relative advantage:

Compatibility:

Perceived Risk:

CHAPTER THIRTEEN
EXAM PRACTICE QUESTIONS

The following questions are designed to test your comprehension of marketing concepts and terminology.

1. An invention is _____, while an improvement is _____.
   A. a change in an existing product, an entirely new type of product
   B. a minor adjustment in an existing product, a significantly better product
   C. an entirely new type of product, a change in an existing product
   D. a technological improvement, a significantly better product
   E. a significantly improved product, a technological advancement

2. A patent is
   A. a model of a product made in limited numbers.
   B. registration and protection of a brand name and logo.
   C. copyright protection for a published product.
   D. a new technology.
   E. the exclusive legal right to make, use, license, and sell an invention.

3. Which of the following is NOT one of the four ways your book suggests companies can use new products to defend and increase a brand's share?
   A. to give a company a foothold in a new category segment
   B. to preempt a market segment
   C. to maintain a firm's position as a product innovator
   D. to help define the corporate culture
   E. to keep overall corporate sales up when other products fail

4. Which of the following is NOT one of the elements which Everett Rogers suggests affect the rate of adoption of a new product idea?
   A. productivity
   B. relative advantage
   C. compatibility
   D. complexity
   E. observables

5. Which of the following is a good internal source of information for new ideas?
   A. customers
   B. suppliers
   C. competition
   D. the sales force
   E. retailers

6. When companies weigh the profitability of a proposed new product idea to decide what level of investment spending to commit to developing a product, it is doing
   A. screening.
   B. concept testing.
   C. product testing.
   D. business analysis
   E. test marketing.

7. Why is concept testing thought to be risky for an invention?
A. the competition may learn about it and start developing its own
B. it makes it much more difficult to locate the breakeven point
C. stakeholders often do not consider it a socially responsible act
D. it increases consumers' perceived risk of purchase
E. competitors may be doing product testing instead

8. The main difference between product testing and test marketing is that test marketing
A. tests the actual product, while product testing just tests ideas.
B. tests the whole marketing mix, not just the product.
C. is national, while product testing is done in limited areas.
D. is done for several products at once, while product testing is for individual products.
E. tests markets, while product testing tests products.

9. The key advantage to a manufacturer from patenting their invention is
A. lower developing costs.
B. legal protection from competitor duplication.
C. guaranteed success.
D. reduced time spent on product testing.
E. shorter development process.

10. After weighing the risks/benefits, what is the next step in new product strategy?
A. product testing
B. marketing mix planning
C. patent approval
D. idea generation
E. test marketing

11. Which of the following is NOT a step in the new product developing process?
A. business analysis
B. advertising post testing
C. idea generation
D. product development testing
E. concept testing

12. The length of the new product development process
A. is always 5 years.
B. depends on product complexity.
C. is determined by product price.
D. is unaffected by competition.
E. depends on profit margin.

13. The last step in new product development process is
A. profit/ loss forecasting.
B. screening.
C. business analysis.
D. concept testing.
E. product launch.

14. In the U.S. a "new" product
A. is significantly better than previous products.
B. must have a patent.
C. must be perceived as new by a group of customers.
D. must not be available overseas.
E. must be test marketed internationally.

15. New products
A. succeed 95% of the time.
B. usually fail due to market misjudgment.
C. are guaranteed success with big budgets for research.
D. will be more profitable if introduced when the product line reaches maturity.
E. are more likely to fail if suppliers are consulted.

The remaining questions are designed to evaluate your ability to apply the text concepts.
16. Saturn's strategy of selling cars using an improved level of service over its competitors, making customers more comfortable with purchasing cars, and offering no-haggle pricing, would best be called a
A. me-too strategy.
B. new product venture strategy.
C. technology advancement strategy.
D. competitive advantage strategy.
E. sweat-free strategy.

17. KLP Thermal Industries was thinking about developing either batter-operated hand warmers or slippers with battery-operated heating units. Given the cost, the fit with existing products, and anticipated consumer response, KLP thermal chose to manufacture the hand warmers for hunters. This process which product to produce is called
A. idea generation.
B. screening.
C. idea testing.
D. product testing.
E. test marketing.

18. The Hears + Corporation has decided that, in order to be profitable, its magazines need to have at least a circulation of 750,000. The company probably determined this through
A. concept testing.
B. marketing research.
C. product testing.
D. breakeven analysis.
E. circulatory analysis.

19. When Frito-Lay came up with an idea for dip-filled chips, they held numerous focus groups with consumers to evaluate the idea. This stage of the new development process is called
A. idea generation.
B. product testing.
C. screening.
D. business analysis.
E. concept testing.

20. When a wine manufacturer develops a new wine, company personnel might be invited to participate in a wine tasting in which they comment on the wine's taste, smell, and color. This is an example of a(n) _____ test.
A. external
B. lab
C. prototype
D. concept
E. in-house

21. Sue received a free bottle of fabric softener in her mailbox. She was asked to use the fabric softener for one month. Then she would be called to answer some questions about the product. The softener came in a white bottle and the label on the container only listed the ingredients of the product and instructions on its use. This is an example of
A. generic testing.
B. intercept testing.
C. secondary research.
D. home placement.
E. test marketing.

22. In order to sell its solar-powered heaters for campers, KELP Thermal Industries introduced them first in markets where KELP products for campers were already well known. As budget permitted, the firm added additional markets. This is an example of
A. geographic introduction.
B. regional inception.
C. market reaction.
D. limited product control
E. product roll out.

23. Of the following, which is the best example of an invention?
A. instant "coffee bags"
B. single serving pudding
C. cented trash liners
D. pink light bulbs
E. CD player

24. Oreo's decision to cover their traditional cookie with fudge represents an
A. improvement.
B. innovation.
C. invention.
D. imitation.
E. prototype.

25. Wendy's offered a "meal deal," bundling a soft drink, sandwich, and fries under one price. Many other fast food restaurants soon followed this strategy. This is an example of _____ product strategy.
A. black market
B. test market.
C. me-too
D. proactive
E. cannibalization

26. The local YMCA polled a cross section of their membership to get suggestions for the design of a new weight training facility. This is an example of
A. screening.
B. test marketing.
C. marketing mix planning.
D. idea generation.
E. prototype testing.

27. Solar powered automobile technology was developed in the 70's. However, auto manufacturers discovered they were not commercially feasible due to high production costs and low sales forecast. This would have been discovered in the _____ stage of new product development process.
A. screening.
B. business analysis
C. test marketing
D. idea generation
E. advertising design

28. Before USA Today publishes a special section they make a rough mockup of what it will look like for their salespeople to use. This model is called a(n)
A. prototype.
B. concept.
C. patent.
D. advertising.
E. throw away.

29. Before Tombstone Pizza launched their product in the southeastern U.S., they tested it in a few key stores and measured customer response. This is an example of a _____ test market.
A. conventional
B. standard
C. controlled
D. benchmark
E. prototype

30. The local university purchased the technology necessary to provide outreach education to potential students unable to come to campus. To facilitate acceptance of this program in the community, the university needed to inform and persuade faculty staff of its advantages. These actions would be considered part of what your text calls
A. product rollout.
B. sell-in.
C. prototype development.
D. test marketing.
E. benchmarking.

Purpose: To increase understanding of the various distribution channel designs.

Instructions: Answer the questions based on one of the cases in your textbook. A product company will be better suited to this exercise due to its longer marketing channel.

The Company:

1. Explain the **Vertical Marketing System** operating for this business. If it is not clearly defined, discuss what you feel would be best. Explain why the alternatives would not work.

2. **Draw** the consumer channel of distribution. See pages 436-437 for descriptions.

The following questions are designed to test your comprehension of marketing concepts and terminology.

1. Distribution channels provide all of the following services EXCEPT
A. manufacturing.
B. carrying inventory.
C. financing.
D. promoting.
E. transportation.

2. A good channel design should consider all of the following EXCEPT
A. distribution objectives.
B. the nature of the product.
C. media availability.
D. the nature of the target market.
E. cost efficiencies.

3. Channel objectives should be stated in terms of the
A. length of the channel.
B. other elements of the marketing mix.
C. desired level of service for the intended target audience.
D. market share desired.
E. cost.

4. Three types of distribution strategies, intensive, selective, or exclusive, can be used to obtain different levels of
A. media coverage.
B. market coverage.
C. target perceptions.
D. product involvement.
E. channel implication.

5. For items like major appliances, stereos, and automobiles, the best distribution strategy would be
A. preference.
B. convenience.
C. intensive.
D. selective.
E. deferred.

6. Generally speaking, the _____ customers, the _____ likely the use of intermediaries.
A. more, more
B. less, more
C. more, less
D. larger, more
E. smaller, less

7. The primary purpose of a just-in-time inventory control system is to allow retailers to
A. meet customer demand by stocking large supplies if inventory.
B. stock only what is needed immediately and quickly order more as needed.
C. assure that inventory is in stock in time for the holiday season.
D. determine who is buying what for future references.
E. track all purchases to determine when they are actually used.

8. A distribution system where channel members remain independent, but agree to work together under the guidance of a channel captain, is called
A. a contractual system.
B. a corporate system.
C. an administered system.
D. an internal system.
E. an external system.

9. Which of the following does NOT describe an intermediary?
A. they are part of the channel of distribution
B. they are basically service companies
C. they facilitate the exchange process
D. they are usually called purchasing agents
E. they are usually not manufacturers

10. A(n) _____ channel uses resellers and wholesalers.
A. indirect
B. direct
C. zero-level
D. services
E. backward

11. Channels of distribution for industrial products
A. are the same as for consumer products.
B. are longer than those for consumer products.
C. are shorter than those for consumer products.
D. use more intermediaries than consumer channels.
E. require less product expertise than consumer channels.

12. Exporters sell products to
A. domestic suppliers.
B. domestic manufacturers.
C. foreign markets.
D. the black markets.
E. intermediaries only.

13. With an effective vertical marketing system
A. channel conflict is reduced.
B. channel conflict is eliminated.
C. scrambled retailing is facilitated.
D. just in time inventory management is jeopardized.
E. franchise agreements are eliminated.

14. A charge by a retailer to a manufacturer to acquire shelf space for a new product is called a
A. internodal fee.
B. slotting allowance.
C. dual channel.
D. containerization commission.
E. warehouse wage.

15. Franchise organizations are part of a _____ vertical marketing system.
A. conventional
B. administered
C. corporate
D. cooperative
E. contractual

The remaining questions are designed to evaluate your ability to apply the text concepts.
16. Hershey's produces millions of cases of chocolate syrup at a plant in Pennsylvania, while Sealtest produces millions of gallons of ice cream at a plant in Michigan, buy consumers want just small quantities of ice cream and chocolate syrup without traveling beyond their local stores. This signifies the importance of _____ in successful marketing.
A. quality control
B. promotion
C. manufacturer coordination
D. distribution
E. marketing myopia

17. Japan sells more products to other countries than it buys from those countries. This puts Japan mostly in the role of
A. insurer.
B. exporter.
C. expediter.
D. importer.
E. impediter.

18. Lotus Development Corporation became irritated with some of its distributors when they sold its 1-2-3 program to mail-order retailers who discounted it by $200 from list price. Lotus felt this pricing hurt the perceived value of its product. This situation is a good example of
A. exclusive distribution violation.
B. dumping.
C. channel conflict
D. vertical marketing system.
E. distribution irritation.

19. Southland Corporation, owner of 7 Eleven, operates its own gasoline refineries. This is an example of
A. an administered system.
B. forward integration.
C. backward integration.
D. a horizontal marketing system.
E. a contractual system.

20. Which of the following products would most likely use water transport?
A. fresh fish
B. convenience products
C. heavy machinery
D. jewelry
E. live animals

21. Honda ships component parts for automobiles in 40-foot containers from Japan to its assembly plant in Marysville, Ohio. The containers are carried by ship to California where they are loaded on trains for the trip to Ohio. This is an example of
A. multiple channels.
B. intermodal transportation.
C. dual distribution.
D. inventory control.
E. distribution intensity.

22. Western Auto is a channel system in which a wholesaler contracts small independent retailers in order to standardize and coordinate buying practices, merchandising programs, and inventory management. Western Auto is an example of
A. an external channel system.
B. an internal channel system.
C. a corporate system.
D. an administered system.
E. a contractual system.

23. When a consumer buys a bouquet of flowers from the nursery that grew them, it is an example of a(n)
A. licensing contract.
B. multi-level channel.
C. intermediary exchange.
D. direct channel.
E. operating system.

24. Some small Pacific island's purchase more goods from other countries than they sell to other countries. This puts them in an _____ role.
A. exporter
B. expatriate
C. intermediary
D. embargo
E. importer

25. "To have it there by 10AM the following day" is an example of a
A. channel objective.
B. product mix.
C. channel length consideration.
D. media goal.
E. franchise agreement.

26. Snickers candy bars are available in supermarkets, convenience store's, vending machines, and service stations. This widespread distribution is classified as
A. extensive.
B. intensive.
C. exclusive.
D. selective.
E. seclusive.

27. For fine wine and expensive perfume, _____ distribution is best.
A. selective
B. inclusive
C. exclusive
D. intermediary
E. convenience

28. A new version of popular the Fritos corn chip will need many wholesalers and retailers to provide market coverage. This is an example of how _____ affects channel design.
A. market density
B. market size
C. market parity
D. market myopia
E. media placement

29. The sub zero temperatures on the South Pole require extreme weather protection. Manufacturers of specially designed gloves to combat frost bite use a direct channel to market to the scientists and expeditionists who frequent this area. This is an example of how market _____ affect channel design.
A. coverage
B. saturation
C. parity
D. myopia
E. density

30. If Fisher Price toys were to open their own retail outlets in malls to exclusively sell their products, they would be engaging in
A. backward integration.
B. cooperative advertising.
C. an administered integration.
D. forward integration.
E. scrambled retailing.

CHAPTER FIFTEEN
APPLICATIONS PROJECT

Purpose: To increase understanding of the elements that marketers must consider when developing a retailing strategy.

Instructions: Discuss the retailing mix for your favorite restaurant. Use pages 476-479 for explanation of the impact of these attributes on the overall image.

Restaurant:_____

1. Service

2. Location

3. Personality and Ambiance

4. Marketing Communication

5. Quality

CHAPTER FIFTEEN
EXAM PRACTICE QUESTIONS

The following questions are designed to test your comprehension of marketing concepts and terminology.

1. A wholesaler
A. links manufacturers with other intermediaries and industrial buyers.
B. sells products directly to customers.
C. is any establishment which advertises "wholesale pricing."
D. is a store which sells to consumers only in large volumes.
E. supplies delivery services to customers.

2. The biggest difference between a merchant wholesaler and an agent or broker is that
A. a merchant wholesaler takes title to the goods while an agent or broker does not.
B. a merchant wholesaler collects commission while an agent or broker does not.
C. a merchant wholesaler specializes while an agent or broker does not.
D. a merchant wholesaler promotes the product while an agent or broker does not.
E. a merchant wholesaler negotiates deals while an agent or broker does not.

3. Drop shippers
A. do not take title to the merchandise they sell.
B. modify most of the merchandise they sell.
C. ship all merchandise from their warehouses directly to customers.
D. do not take possession of the merchandise they sell.
E. sell goods on consignment.

4. An agent who sells two or more related product lines from noncompeting manufacturers in a specific geographic territory is called a
A. drop shipper.
B. commission merchant.
C. merchant wholesaler.
D. selling agent.
E. manufacturer's representative.

5. Retailers typically add value in any of the following ways EXCEPT
A. product packaging.
B. cheaper prices.
C. convenient location.
D. product variety.
E. personal assistance.

6. Depth of selection in a retail store refers to
A. selection within a product line.
B. the number of advertised brands carried.
C. the number of different types of products available.
D. the selection available within a certain price range.
E. the length of store shelves.

7. The wheel of retailing is a
A. life cycle theory of retailing.
B. location decision theory for retailers.
C. guide to measuring retail success.
D. determinant of scrambling strategies
E. classification scheme for retail stores.

8. A store that brings discounting to brand and designer fashions is called
A. a supermarket.
B. a franchise.
C. a department store.
D. an off-price store.
E. a convenience store.

9. An agent
A. is an intermediary.
B. takes title to the goods they sell.
C. is outside the channel of distribution.
D. is only responsible for shipping.
E. works exclusively for wholesalers.

10. A broker
A. is NOT an intermediary.
B. takes title to the goods they sell.
C. represents a specific manufacturer.
D. specializes in product lines.
E. works exclusively for the seller.

11. The "customer" to a retailer is
A. the manufacturer.
B. the final user.
C. wholesalers.
D. other retailers.
E. channel intermediaries.

12. A(n) _____ mix for a retailer is similar to product mix for a manufacturer.
A. retail
B. inventory
C. merchandise
D. depth
E. jobber

13. Retailers whose primary advantage is time and place utility are categorized as
A. specialty stores.
B. discount supermarkets.
C. rack jobbers.
D. convenience stores.
E. superstores.

14. When customers group together to take advantage of volume purchasing it is called a
A. superstore.
B. franchise organization.
C. corporate marketing system.
D. cooperative.
E. wholesale league.

15. Which of the following is NOT part of the retailing mix?
A. location
B. product packaging
C. store ambiance
D. merchandise selection
E. price range

The remaining questions are designed to evaluate your ability to apply the text concepts.

16. Cannondale Corporation, which makes mountain bikes, now distributes its own products in the Japanese market. The company functions in Japan as a
A. merchant wholesaler.
B. manufacturer-wholesaler.
C. broker.
D. agent.
E. rack jobber.

17. Mitsubishi Corporation often acts as both a purchasing and sales agent for the companies it represents and handles both imports and exports. In these roles, Mitsubishi functions as a
A. mitsunomi.
B. foreign franchisor.
C Japanese superstore.
D. merchant broker.
E. trading company.

18. Mrs. Field's Cookies sells only cookies (along with some drinks and related baked goods). This store would be referred to as a
A. single-line store.
B. scrambled marketing store.
C. department store.
D. monitored store.
E. related store.

19. At Sam's Club, you can buy everything from television sets to electric blankets, from tires to bubble gum, and from leather jackets to file cabinets. What is the term used to describe this strategy?
A. discount marketing
B. margin merchandising
C. scrambled marketing
D. aggregated retailing
E. inventory turnover marketing

20. Benetton, Baskin Robbins and Louis Vuitton all focus on one particular product type. They are examples of
A. discount stores.
B. convenience stores.
C. supermarkets.
D. specialty stores.
E. department stores.

21. Toys R Us is a good example of a
A. department store.
B. hypermarket.
C. cooperative.
D. category killer.
E. convenience store.

22. A hypermarket is
A. a store which offers brand merchandise at discount prices.
B. a store which offers a selection of convenience items and keeps long hours.
C. a large store which offers broad product lines in food and general merchandise.
D. a large retail store selling a variety of non-food product lines.
E. a store that focuses narrowly on one product or line.

23. When you give up going home for the holidays, so you can stay on campus and work, the value of what you're giving up is called
A. marginal cost.
B. opportunity cost.
C. credit opportunity.
D. slotting allowance.
E. sacrifice expense.

24. Forest wholesalers buy several acres of wood from lumbermills and resell them by the truckload to home improvement centers. This is an example of
A. scrambled merchandising.
B. franchising.
C. target segmenting.
D. lot splitting.
E. rack jobbing.

25. Which of the following should have the greatest merchandise mix breadth?
A. Kenney's shoe store
B. Bresler's Ice Cream shop
C. Midas Muffler shop
D. Toy's R Us
E. 7-Eleven convenience store

26. Which of the following should have the greatest product line depth?
A. Discount Auto Parts
B. K-mart
C. 7-Eleven convenience store
D. McDonald's
E. Texaco Food Mart

27. K-mart and Target, both large retail stores selling a variety of product lines, are considered
A. supermarkets.
B. department stores.
C. convenience stores.
D. single line stores.
E. superstores.

28. Staples, Bookstop and Home Depot are all large volume, single-line stores called
A. superstores.
B. department stores.
C. supermarkets.
D. scrambled shops.
E. convenience stores.

29. Which of the following would be categorized as a supermarket?
A. a 7-Eleven convenience store
B. a Winn-Dixie franchise
C. a McDonald's location
D. a Sam's Warehouse Club
E. a Bresler's Ice Cream shop

30. Subway Sandwich shops were able to expand rapidly by contracting with individuals to operate Subway locations nationwide. This reduced the capital outlay for the parent company, while generating monthly revenue from contract fees. This is an example of
A. the wheel of retailing.
B. a cooperative.
C. a superstore.
D. exporting.
E. franchising.

CHAPTER SIXTEEN
APPLICATIONS PROJECT

Purpose: To distinguish among the four C's of pricing.

Instructions: Briefly list the price influences in each area of the four C's for the two companies listed. Contrast the changes in impact of each area on the two distinctive organizations. Consult the integrative cases in the back of your text for pricing information.

<u>The Body Shop</u>   <u>Harley Davidson</u>

1. Costs:
   Fixed:

   Variable:

2. Customer Demand:
   Elasticity of Demand:

3. Competitive Influences:
   Market Structure:

   Competitive Pricing Policy:

4. Controls:
   Which agencies have regulatory power?

CHAPTER SIXTEEN
EXAM PRACTICE QUESTIONS

The following questions are designed to test your comprehension of marketing concepts and terminology.

1. According to your text, the "four C's" which determine how prices are set are
A. cost, competition, communication, and centrality.
B. competition, controls, communication, and creation.
C. customer demand, controls, creation, and consumption.
D. cost, competition, communication, and collusion.
E. cost, customer demand, competition, and controls.

2. The primary reason that cost-plus pricing is not used today as much as it used to be is
A. increased consumer choice.
B. declining profit margins.
C. increasing costs.
D. higher quality products.
E. more benefit strengths.

3. When demand is quite responsive to changes in price, it is called
A. competitive demand.
B. elastic demand.
C. stable demand.
D. cost-based demand.
E. inelastic demand.

4. A demand curve is a graphic representation of
A. the effect of quality on price.
B. the effect of a change in price on the number of units.
C. the effect of a change in quality on the number of units sold.
D. the impact of marketing communication on demand.
E. the effectiveness of a particular advertisement.

5. U.S. laws forbid all of the following price practices EXCEPT:
A. competitive pricing
B. price-fixing
C. price discrimination
D. predatory pricing
E. deceptive price advertising

6. Setting an artificially low price for the purpose of containing or driving a competitor out of the market is an illegal practice known as
A. price discrimination.
B. predatory pricing.
C. deceptive pricing.
D. resale price maintenance.
E. price-fixing.

7. Bait-and-switch pricing is setting a price which
A. is low to attract customers who are then persuaded to trade up.
B. is not offered consistently to all buyers.
C. is based on a fictitious "original" price.
D. is claimed to be a wholesale price when it really is not.
E. is artificially high to make the product seem higher quality than it is.

8. The percentage of revenue that remains after both fixed and variable costs have been subtracted is called
A. average unit revenue.
B. marginal revenue.
C. markup ratio.
D. cost-plus revenue.
E. profit margin.

9. The level of satisfaction a product creates as compared to the product's cost to the consumer determines
A. break-even.
B. value.
C. elasticity.
D. fixed cost.
E. profit.

10. The two major types of costs are
A. primary and selective.
B. profit and marginal.
C. operating and variable.
D. fixed and elastic.
E. fixed and variable.

11. The type of cost that remains constant in the short run, regardless of production, is a _____ cost.
A. fixed
B. variable
C. profit
D. marginal
E. primary

12. Total costs
A. are based on profit.
B. exclude operating expenses.
C. are equal to the sum of fixed and variable costs.
D. equal marginal cost.
E. are equal to the sum of profit and overhead.

13. Price discrimination
A. is legal in the Northeastern U.S.
B. is legal only for sole proprietorships.
C. occurs when customers are charged different prices for the same products.
D. is commonly referred to as monopoly pricing.
E. sets a universal price for the entire industry.

14. The point at which total costs equal total revenue and profit is zero is called
A. marginal setpoint.
B. point of elasticity.
C. price ceiling.
D. break-even.
E. variable margin.

15. Price elastic demand indicates
A. there are no substitute goods.
B. your market is brand insistent.
C. well-differentiated products offerings.
D. a price-insensitive market.
E. a price-sensitive market.

The remaining questions are designed to evaluate your ability to apply the text concepts.

16. While a movie theater may be able to attract only 50 viewers for a matinee performance if tickets sell for $6.00, it can often attract 300 or more people in the evening for the same ticket price. This phenomenon is called
A. price precipitation.
B. changing unit analysis.
C. price variation theory.
D. redefining demand.
E. shifting the demand curve.

17. When Dole lowered the price on its bananas, Chiquita almost immediately did the same, because the banana market most closely resembles a market structure of
A. oligopoly.
B. monopoly.
C. poligopoly.
D. pure competition.
E. monopolistic competition.

18. When the OPEC countries agree to price levels at which they will set the price of crude oil, this is an example of
A. price fixing.
B. deceptive pricing.
C. resale price maintenance.
D. predatory pricing.
E. price discrimination.

19. When retailers in the community agree on the price they will charge for Nintendo games, it is an example of
A. vertical price-fixing.
B. price discrimination.
C. fair-trade pricing.
D. horizontal price-fixing.
E. predatory pricing.

20. An Italian leather manufacturer that sold its eelskin leather in the U.S. markets for less than it sold the leather in Italy would be guilty of
A. horizontal price-fixing.
B. dumping.
C. price collusion.
D. resale price maintenance.
E. international price-fixing.

21. A retailer advertises that its ski parkas have a suggested retail price of $75, but that it will sell them for $35. The store is guilty of _____ unless other stores in the trade area offer comparable parkas for $75.
A. predatory pricing
B. resale price maintenance
C. deceptive pricing
D. vertical price-fixing
E. horizontal price-fixing

22. If the Foot Locker puts a pair of shoes which normally retails for $80 on sale for "25% off," its _____ would be $20.
A. markup
B. markdown
C. marginal reduction
D. unit loss
E. marginal loss

23. Which of the following is an example of a fixed cost to a college bookstore?
A. shopping bags
B. notebook paper
C. rent
D. charge receipts
E. highlighters

24. Of the following, which is most likely to be a variable cost to a drive-in movie theater?
A. insurance
B. real estate taxes
C. Chamber of Commerce dues
D. movie royalties
E. popcorn

25. When one fast-food restaurant lowers their price, college students generally switch brands to take advantage of the lower price. In this case, demand would be considered
A. price inelastic.
B. price elastic.
C. price survival.
D. selectively loyal.
E. fixed.

26. Price increases on life supporting medicine/treatment faces ethical considerations since many times there are no substitutes for these products. The demand would be defined as _____ in these cases.
A. price inelastic
B. price elastic
C. price survival
D. fixed
E. primary cost

27. Based on actual experience and market research, Jackie knows the most her customers will pay for a bouquet of flowers is $30. This is called a
A. fixed demand.
B. fixed cost.
C. price ceiling.
D. price margin.
E. profit margin.

28. When Jill, a local home economics teacher, shops for recipe ingredients to be used at school, she always chooses the less expensive without any consideration of quality. Jill is treating her ingredients as
A. speciality goods.
B. impulsive items.
C. luxury products.
D. commodities.
E. heterogeneous shopping products.

29. Nike has warned retailers that if they discount their products more than 10% below manufacturer suggested price, they will no longer include them in Nike's distribution channel. This pricing is called
A. predatory pricing.
B. price discrimination.
C. minimum pricing.
D. price-fixing.
E. resale price maintenance.

30. Adam sold ice cream bars on campus every Friday. His total costs for the day were $50. This week he sold 75 bars at $2 each. What was his profit for this week?
A. $100
B. $50
C. $75
D. $150
E. $25

CHAPTER SEVENTEEN
APPLICATIONS PROJECT

Purpose: To further understand customer-oriented pricing strategies.

Instructions: List an original example of a service product for which the listed plan of action would be appropriate and effective. List another where it would be ineffective. Use yourself as the target market. Briefly describe your reasoning for each.

CUSTOMER-ORIENTED STRATEGIES

	Effective	Ineffective

Skim pricing:

Penetration pricing:

Psychological pricing:

    image pricing:

    price lining:

Value-Based pricing:

Price Bundling:

The following questions are designed to test your comprehension of marketing concepts and terminology.

1. The goals a company wants to accomplish in order to protect and increase profits are called
A. pricing objectives.
B. financial directions.
C. price points.
D. corporate mission.
E. financial returns.

2. Reformulating the product so it costs less to produce or reducing the size of a product are tactics companies use to help achieve
A. a cost advantage.
B. pricing containment.
C. a stable price.
D. customer demand.
E. increased stock turnover.

3. Cost-oriented pricing strategies are based primarily on
A. the external needs of customers.
B. the demand of competition.
C. the internal needs of the company.
D. the demand of suppliers.
E. the needs of corporate executives.

4. A _____ pricing strategy is used when the seller is reluctant to bid on a government contract because of the many uncontrollable factors involved that could result in loss instead of profit.
A. cost-plus-fixed-fee
B. margin
C. reference
D. profit plus
E. target-return

5. How long a price-skimming strategy can work effectively for a company depends mostly on
A. the barriers to entry which limit competition.
B. how long the product has been on the market.
C. the profit level achieved by the firm.
D. the cost to produce the product.
E. the management abilities of company executives.

6. Products whose prices cannot be changed much because of deeply held customer reference values must be priced according to a _____ strategy.
A. contrast pricing
B. image pricing
C. customary pricing
D. price bundling
E. price penetration

7. Examples of value-based pricing include all of the following EXCEPT:
A. value-in-use pricing
B. EVC pricing
C. everyday-low-prices
D. reference pricing
E. price bundling

8. Promotional pricing can often lead to damaging
A. advertising battles.
B. image pricing.
C. price escalations.
D. price wars.
E. price bidding.

9. Which of the following is NOT one of the three C's generally addressed by pricing objectives?
A. costs
B. competition
C. consumption
D. consumer demand
E. A and C

10. Markups are used primarily in a _____ pricing strategy.
A. demand analysis
B. sales forecast
C. experience curve
D. profit plus
E. cost plus

11. Which of the following conditions support the USR of a target-return pricing strategy?
A. supply exceeds demand
B. price inelastic demand
C. market penetration objectives
D. competition-oriented objectives
E. products perceived as commodities

12. Sometimes referred to as a "learning or growth" curve, _____ curve pricing relies on the assumption that variable costs will decrease as sales volume increases.
A. experience
B. profit
C. target
D. ROI
E. elasticity

13. Under which of the following market conditions would penetration pricing NOT be effective?
A. price-sensitive customers
B. intense competition
C. highly differentiated products
D. widespread availability of substitute goods
E. customers perceive products as shopping goods

14. Pricing bread at .19 to build store traffic is using _____ pricing.
A. image
B. EDLP
C. EVC
D. bid
E. loss leader

15. Often discounts are used by manufacturers to facilitate the exchange process with market intermediaries. Which of the following does NOT accomplish that objective?
A. quantity discounts
B. seasonal discounts
C. promotional allowances
D. pro forma rebates
E. cash discounts

The remaining questions are designed to evaluate your ability to apply the text concepts.
16. If XYZ Company wants to make a $10,000 profit selling 1000 widgets and has a fixed cost of $10,000 and a unit variable costs of $10 each widget, what price should the company set using target-return pricing?
A. $10
B. $20
C. $30
D. $100
E. $120

17. When Pepsi introduced Crystal Pepsi, the original version of Crystal, the company introduced the product at prices below retail prices of other Pepsi and Coke products to attempt to build market share for Crystal Pepsi. This is an example of
A. skim pricing.
B. image pricing.
C. value-in-use pricing.
D. penetration pricing.
E. price lining.

18. Men's suits are commonly sold at certain price points like $129.95, $179.95, and $249.95. This is an example of
A. customary pricing.
B. price lining.
C. blocked pricing.
D. penetration pricing.
E. competitive-advantage pricing.

19. Target discount stores say that all their prices are already as low as they can set them, so they don't have regular sales on selected items. The stores appear to be using
A. economic-value-to-the-customer (EVC) pricing.
B. everyday low pricing.
C. value-in-use pricing.
D. target return pricing.
E. price bundling.

20. If Smithson Electronics knows that customers will get approximately $100 more benefits from its appliance and also pay about $100 less in maintenance over the life of the product, then the company should be able to charge about $200 more for its product. This is an example of
A. economic daily level price (EDLP) pricing.
B. price bundling.
C. cost plus pricing.
D. economic-value-to-the-customer (EVC) pricing.
E. benefit additive pricing.

21. Mont Blanc charges a premium price for its fountain pen ($250) because customers view its products as built-to-last status symbols. In terms of its industry, Mont Blanc is a
A. loss leader.
B. price follower.
C. competitive pricer.
D. price topper.
E. price leader.

22. When the U.S. Department of Defense decides to build additional military vehicles, it generally will ask a small group of defense contractors to submit sealed proposals detailing how they will meet a set of specifications and what they will charge to build the vehicles. The contract is then awarded to the lowest-priced qualified bidder. This process of pricing is called
A. competitive-bid pricing.
B. loss-leader pricing.
C. contractual process pricing.
D. price lining.
E. undercut pricing.

23. John invested $10,000 in his skate rental business. At the end of his first year he wanted to calculate a ratio to compare his net income with total equity. The formula he needs is
A. inventory turnover.
B. return on share.
C. markup.
D. return on investment.
E. profit margin.
24. Many service companies, in an attempt to improve demand management, use USR pricing strategies to balance out fluctuations. This would be accomplished by
A. pricing low at peak times and pricing high when demand is lowest.
B. pricing high at peak times and pricing low when demand is lowest.
C. consistent use of cost-plus pricing.
D. pricing highest when competition is intense and lowering price as competition decreases.
E. a skim pricing policy.

25. When Rollerblades first introduced their inline skates to the market, they were considered new and innovative and had no competition. The best pricing strategy, given these market conditions, was
A. luxury pricing.
B. penetration pricing.
C. experience-curve pricing.
D. markup pricing.
E. skim pricing.

26. Cologne is priced based on the type of customer targeted and the perception of the product created through promotional efforts. This strategy is called
A. image pricing.
B. penetration pricing.
C. experience-curve pricing.
D. markup pricing.
E. skim pricing.

27. Before launching their new product line of Children's outerwear, Lands End conducted market research to determine the price points customers assume to pay for these products. They then set prices based on this data. This is _____ pricing.
A. experience curve
B. research table
C. penetration
D. skim
E. reference

28. Cathy wanted to sell bouquets of flowers at the weekly school flea market. She noticed that her competition sold their bouquets for $5. Remembering the concept of _____ pricing, she priced her bouquets at $4.99 to make them appear to be less expensive.
A. skim
B. odd
C. price lining
D. markup
E. commodity

29. The concept behind Rooms-To-Go is called
A. price bundling.
B. skim pricing.
C. dual pricing.
D. target audience pricing.
E. EDLP.

30. The Frolicking Frog toy store has to monitor the pricing strategy of the industry leader, Toys 'R Us, and adjust their prices accordingly. The Frolicking Frog would be considered a
A. price leader.
B. price marcher.
C. price reactor.
D. price follower.
E. bid pricer.

CHAPTER EIGHTEEN
APPLICATIONS PROJECT

Purpose: To gain insight into the types of advertising and media strategy used in marketing communication.

Instructions: Select a print advertisement from any source. Evaluate your selection by answering the questions listed.

1. Identify the target audience:

2. Type of Advertising (Circle **one** and explain why.)

      Brand

      Corporate

      Business-to-Business

      Retail

3. Hierarchy of Effects (Pick the **one** that most accurately describes the intended effect and explain)

      Attention

      Interest

      Desire

      Action

4. Media Rationale WHY did your ad appear in the media you found it in?

      Media:

CHAPTER EIGHTEEN
EXAM PRACTICE QUESTIONS

The following questions are designed to test your comprehension of marketing concepts and terminology.

1. Messages which are implied by other parts of the marketing mix, like price, distribution method, and the product are called
A. inferred messages.
B. planned messages.
C. reversal messages.
D. catatonic messages.
E. covert messages.

2. Those marketing messages which have the most impact on potential customers, but over which marketers have virtually no control, are called
A. inferred messages.
B. planned messages.
C. public messages.
D. unplanned messages.
E. impact messages.

3. When a company conducts a contact point analysis, it is most likely analyzing
A. all occasions when consumers came in contact with a particular brand.
B. all interactions between sales clerks and customers in stores which carry a product.
C. the strength of relationships with current customers.
D. the ratios achieved by a telemarketing sales staff.
E. the response ratio for a mail order catalog.

4. Integrated marketing communications means
A. offering an integrated package of price, distribution, and product.
B. creating an advertising campaign which integrates price levels into the message.
C. selecting media which all integrate the company's message to a single target market.
D. coordinating all of the messages and media used to influence value perceptions.
E. reorganizing so a company's salespeople work for the advertising managers.

5. Impact of the communication is easiest to measure for
A. advertising and packaging.
B. public relations and advertising.
C. personal selling and public relations.
D. advertising and sales promotion.
E. sales promotion and direct marketing.

6. Advertising is any
A. communication of a message designed to stimulate buying.
B. unpaid form of presentation of ideas.
C. message about a product or company transmitted by the mass media.
D. paid form of non-personal presentation of ideas in the mass media.
E. persuasive message transmitted by a company.

7. A type of corporate advertising which communicates a company's views on environmental, social, business, or other issues is called
A. brand advertising.
B. social advertising.
C. advocacy advertising.
D. cooperative advertising.
E. business advertising.

8. Retail advertising is advertising which
A. creates and nurtures positive attitudes towards the company.
B. is directed at people who buy or influence the purchase for a company.
C. establishes product personality or image and builds product equity.
D. is designed primarily to attract customers into a store.
E. retailers place with support material or reimbursement from the manufacturer.

9. Which of the following is NOT an element of the marketing communication model?
A. sender
B. receiver
C. transmitter
D. media
E. encoding

10. The key advantage of public relations as a marketing communication tool is the
A. attention getting ability.
B. sales generation capacity.
C. perception of credibility.
D. market targeting ability.
E. behavior orientation.

11. Impulse goods rely on the attention-getting ability of
A. packaging.
B. pricing.
C. brand management.
D. personal selling.
E. publicity.

12. After marketing objectives are determined, the next step is that _____ must be selected.
A. noise reducers
B. target audience
C. message execution
D. message coordination
E. strategies

13. One of advertising's major weakness is
A. audience reach.
B. message repetition ability.
C. its effect on brand image.
D. high level of audience avoidance.
E. ability to position a brand.

14. Advertising in which the manufacturer provides advantage materials/reimbursement to a retailer is _____ advertising.
A. publicity
B. cooperative
C. corporate
D. public service
E. retroactive

15. Preemptive advertising
A. stakes out a position before anyone else can claim it.
B. uses alternative media.
C. does not encounter noise.
D. replaces the need for feedback.
E. is used for products with decreasing market share to cut costs.

The remaining questions are designed to evaluate your ability to apply the text concepts.

16. The conflicts some people experience when they see a controversial Benetton ad would be an example of _____ in the traditional communication model.
A. encoding
B. noise
C. media
D. perpetration
E. cognition

17. Which of the following would most likely be an IMC objective?
A. price the product lower to capture larger market share
B. place the product in discount stores as well as supermarkets
C. capture 30% market share by the end of five years
D. generate trial among 35% of the target market by year end
E. increase sales by 50%

18. If the public relations department of a company is trying to establish the company as a good corporate citizen, but the company's product is being packaged with a lot of wasteful packaging, the packaging message would probably get in the way of the public relations message. This is an example of
A. noise.
B. encoding.
C. integration.
D. advertising.
E. interception.

19. When Cambell Company airs ads that say "Soup is Good Food," the company is using primarily
A. selective demand advertising.
B. secondary demand advertising.
C. principle advertising.
D. primary demand advertising.
E. cooperative advertising.

20. A Folgers coffee crystal ad emphasized how a cup of coffee made using its coffee crystals was much darker and more robust than coffee made from other brands of instant coffee. This is an example of _____ advertising.
A. cooperative
B. derived demand
C. business to business
D. primary demand
E. selective demand

21. Which statement represents an advertising-to-sales ratio?
A. advertising for XYZ company created an additional $25 million in sales last year
B. the XYZ ad cost $2000 and generated $10,000 in additional sales; a ratio of 1:5
C. each ad for XYZ company costs the company about 2 units in sales
D. XYZ company spends 1% of sales on advertising
E. advertising is 3% of XYZ company's marketing budget

22. The makers of Cadillac have discovered that, while most consumers are aware of the Cadillac brand name, there is little interest in the car by many consumers. They have decided, therefore, that advertising objectives need to move beyond attention and awareness to achieve interest and desire. These decisions seem to be based on
A. advertising to sales ratios.
B. a hierarchy of effects model.
C. task objective methods.
D. a needs-motivation model.
E. advertising ratio analysis.

23. You have been hired to write a radio ad for your fraternity's benefit softball game. You are playing the role of
A. media.
B. encoder.
C. decoder.
D. sender.
E. source.

24. Eric called some friends and went to the movie he saw advertised in the newspaper. His action is an example of
A. feedback.
B. noise.
C. encoding
D. sending.
E. sales promotion.

25. Pillsbury includes their logo and trademark "Dough Boy" in all communications with customers. This would be an example of
A. INC.
B. IMP.
C. ICC.
D. AMC.
E. IMC.

26. The local sandwich shop relies on coupons, contests, and other short-term techniques to increase sales. This tool is called
A. advertising.
B. public relations.
C. sales promotion.
D. noise.
E. publicity.

27. Every year, the marketing manager for Kaplan Review Courses starts the marketing communication planning process fresh, as if no previous promotion existed. This type of plan is referred to as a(n)_____ plan.
A. annualized
B. negative start
C. media bound
D. zero based
E. optimum sum

28. When Tropicana places advertising to communicate product freshness and availability, it is using _____ advertising.
A. referral
B. brand
C. corporate
D. cooperative
E. retail

29. Weyerhauser's magazine ads that inform the public of its forestation programs are an example of _____ advertising.
A. referral
B. brand
C. corporate
D. cooperative
E. retail

30. Mead Products uses trade journals to persuade organizations with large office staffs to use their paper products. This is an example of _____ advertising.
A. corporate
B. business to business
C. retail
D. brand
E. public service

CHAPTER NINETEEN
APPLICATIONS PROJECT

Purpose: To increase understanding of the strengths and weaknesses of sales promotion tools.

Instructions: Choose a product from those used as examples (boxes, cases) in your text. Define target market, then explain why you would, or would not, use the following seven sales promotion tools, give examples of those you would use.

Product:

Target Market:

1. Samples?

   Delivery method of the sample?

2. Couponing?

3. Premiums?

4. Contests or sweepstakes?

5. Refunds or Rebates?

6. Point of Purchase Materials?

7. Trade Promotions?

The following questions are designed to test your comprehension of marketing concepts and terminology.

1. Which of the following statements about PR is true?
A. PR is easily controlled by the public relations specialist
B. the primary objective of PR is to maximize brand awareness at any cost
C. PR generally generates messages with high credibility
D. PR can be used to avoid hard to reach target audiences
E. media costs for PR can be high

2. Sales promotion provides
A. an extra reason for the customer to buy or respond.
B. the psychological environment for selling.
C. information about the product which helps a consumer to decide.
D. media attention for a product.
E. improved product quality.

3. Sales promotion has overtaken advertising in most marketing mixes because
A. its results are immediately discernible.
B. it has a higher image with customers.
C. it reaches more people than advertising.
D. it is less expensive than advertising.
E. it is best for building long-term brand equity.

4. The marketing communication tool listed below for which it is easiest to measure results is
A. advertising.
B. sales promotion.
C. public relations.
D. distribution.
E. packaging.

5. Bonus packs are an example of a technique used as part of a _____ strategy.
A. continuity
B. penetration
C. publicity
D. loading
E. authorization

6. A premium is a
A. free gift or reward which requires no purchase and carries a reminder message.
B. product offered free of charge as a reward for purchasing something else.
C. a display designed to give a brand or product line extra in-store exposure
D. a sales promotion that promotes two purchases together.
E. a sales promotion that uses one brand to promote another non-competing brand.

7. A dealer loader is
A. a product offered free of charge as a reward for purchasing something else.
B. a display designed to give a brand or product line extra in-store exposure.
C. a sales promotion that promotes two products together.
D. a sales promotion that uses one brand to promote another non-competing brand.
E. an item of value to retailers that is offered to encourage them to use a display.

8. A trade show is
A. a show put on by retailers to help consumers decide to buy products from them.
B. an exhibition to display a variety of consumer items to interest consumers.
C. an exhibition where firms display their products to potential industry buyers.
D. a show put on by retailers to convince manufacturers to display products with them.
E. a fashion show with strict entry requirements for qualified customers.

9. The public relations portion of marketing communication includes all of the following EXCEPT
A. publicity.
B. newsletters.
C. pricing policy.
D. event sponsorship.
E. goodwill building activities.

10. Which of the following is NOT a target audience for public relations activities?
A. competitors
B. employees
C. suppliers
D. shareholders
E. customers

11. Which of the following would be considered collateral material?
A. press conference
B. brand advertising
C. cash discounts
D. credit policy
E. sales brochure

12. PR is more effective than sales promotion
A. in creating short-term sales increases.
B. influencing immediate buying behavior.
C. with a easily influenced audience such as children.
D. in generating a perception of credibility.
E. in utilizing coupons and premiums as promotional tools.

13. Which of the following is best for successful cross promotion between two organizations?
A. competing brands
B. similar target markets
C. product substitutability
D. different levels within the channels
E. same price points

14. According to your text, crisis management includes all of the following EXCEPT
A. issuing a quick response.
B. facilitating comprehensive information exchange.
C. offering a denial of negligence.
D. playing an active role in crisis resolution.
E. maintaining an interactive role with the media.

15. When compared to advertising, sales promotion is better
A. at reaching more people.
B. at building brand image.
C. at contributing to long-term growth.
D. at enhancing product positioning.
E. at stimulating immediate response.

The remaining questions are designed to evaluate your ability to apply the text concepts.

16. When Ocean Spray introduced its new flavored lemonades, the company sent a packet of information about the development of the product and its features to new-product editors at newspapers and magazines around the country. This packet is an example of
A. a sales promotion.
B. a media tour.
C. an authorization.
D. a press kit.
E. a media promotion.

17. If 20% of U.S. travelers who fly by airplane each year fly on United Airlines, then 20% is United's
A. authorization.
B. penetration.
C. loading.
D. market attainment.
E. comportion.

18. United's frequent flyer program which offers free flights to customers who travel a certain number of miles, is an example of
A. a sales contest.
B. a trade promotion.
C. an authorization program.
D. a loading program.
 E. a continuity program.

19. When Frookies offered large trade allowances to Toys 'R Us and various supermarkets to carry the company's new healthy cookies, the company was probably using these allowances primarily to secure
A. brand authorization.
B. brand loyalty.
C. product advertising.
D. media coverage.
E. customer awareness.

20. After Mary bought the can of Pringle's chips, she mailed its proof of purchase to the manufacturer and received a check for $1.29. This is an example of a
A. discount.
B. rebate.
C. coupon.
D. sample.
E. premium.

21. When companies send out free VCR's or portable televisions with the company name imprinted on them to key decision makers in companies they wish to influence, they are using _____ as a sales promotion tool.
A. cross promotions
B. tie ins
C. specialties
D. premiums
E. bonuses

22. When McDonald's sold Babes in Toyland and other Orion Pictures' videotapes for $7.99 during the holiday season in 1992, it was an example of the two companies' use of
A. joint advertising.
B. a tie-in promotion.
C. specialty items.
D. premium pricing.
E. bonus selling.

23. The college newspaper chose not to run Brian's news release on his fraternity's golf tournament. The fraternity blamed the _____ for their decision not to run the story.
A. publicity patrons
B. media gatekeepers
C. advertising tour group
D. media tour group
E. press conference

24. When Jeff Katzenburg resigned from Walt Disney, Disney initiated a _____ to announce the event.
A. press conference
B. media tour
C. press kit
D. public service announcement
E. collateral conference

25. Brooks Brothers offered customers free alterations on any Brooks Brothers charge card purchase. This is an example of a _____ promotion.
A. trade
B. consumer
C. publicity
D. stakeholder
E. public

26. Dole offered any retailer who increased sales of Dole products by 20% or more an all-expense paid trip to Hawaii. This is a _____ promotion strategy.
A. consumer
B. allowance
C. intermediary
D. trade
E. bribery

27. Snackwells needed to stimulate impulse buying for their new chocolate fudge cookie. The best consumer sales promotion tool would be
A. publicity.
B. public service announcements.
C. sales contests.
D. trade allowances.
E. Point of purchase displays.

28. To counteract a competitor's advertising blitz in the Texas market, Tide repackaged their product in that market with an extra 12oz. This sales promotion is called
A. trade avoidance.
B. promotional allowance.
C. bonus pack.
D. rebate.
E. premium trade.

29. Thom McAnn shoes ran a _____ coupon announcing a savings of $10 on any shoe purchase at any Thom McAnn outlet.
A. retailer-sponsored
B. manufacturer-sponsored
C. trade-sponsored
D. sampling
E. bonus pack

30. As Gary left the state fair, he was given a free pack of Bubble Yum's new tangerine gum to try. This practice is called _____ and is used primarily with new product introductions.
A. free publicity
B. consumer rebate
C. retailer coupon
D. bonus packaging
E. sampling

CHAPTER TWENTY
APPLICATIONS PROJECT

Purpose: To increase understanding of the strengths and strategies of direct response marketing.

Instructions: Discuss the usefulness and applicability of the direct marketing strengths listed below to your university/college. Use pp.626-629 for clarification of concepts..

Convenience:

Precision Targeting:

Interactivity:

Measurability:

Marketing-Mix Efficiencies:

Instructions: Discuss the disadvantages of direct response from the buyers (student) standpoint.

CHAPTER TWENTY
EXAM PRACTICE QUESTIONS

The following questions are designed to test your comprehension of marketing concepts and terminology.

1. A system of marketing that integrates ordinarily separate marketing-mix elements to sell directly to both consumers and other businesses, bypassing retail stores and personal sales calls, is called
A. direct marketing.
B. retail marketing.
C. wholesale marketing.
D. approach marketing.
E. integrated marketing.

2. Direct marketing is one type of transaction. The other two major types of transactions are
A. telephone and wholesale.
B. retail and telephone.
C. retail and personal selling.
D. personal selling and mail.
E. mail and store.

3. One of the major strengths of using direct marketing for a small, well-defined market is
A. a low-cost waste percentage.
B. cost commonalities.
C. homogeneous promotion.
D. message verification.
E. fixed results.

4. Which of the following is NOT a way in which direct marketing creates marketing-mix efficiencies?
A. lower media and selling cost
B. alternative distribution channels
C. a second sales force
D. inventory management
E. product quality improvements

5. Which of the following is NOT usually a direct marketing disadvantage from a buyer's point of view?
A. inconvenience
B. relinquishing privacy
C. not having a chance to see or test a product
D. dealing with businesses the customer never sees
E. additional expense

6. All of the following are criteria used by direct marketers in evaluating mailing lists EXCEPT
A. urgency of the offer responded to previously
B. frequency of direct-response purchases
C. recency of last direct-response purchases
D. amount of money spent on last direct-response purchase
E. from what product category a product was purchased.

7. Direct mail is an advertising
A. campaign.
B. message.
C. monitor.
D. medium.
E. supplement.

8. Audiotext is
A. use of automatic dialing to prospects followed by a recorded message.
B. use of electronic mail to reach prospective customers.
C. a system which sends audio signals out over phone lines to activate fax machines.
D. a system of 800 or 900 number hotlines with recorded messages.
E. a database system transmitted to personal computers via phone lines.

9. Without _____, direct marketing would not be successful.
A. retailers
B. a database
C. mass media
D. a salesperson
E. wholesalers

10. Which of the following is NOT a "user" of direct marketing techniques?
A. retail clothing stores
B. non-profit organizations
C. book and record clubs
D. financial services companies
E. government purchases

11. All of the following are strengths of direct marketing EXCEPT
A. low cost.
B. measurability.
C. precision targeting.
D. underactivity.
E. convenience.

12. Because many direct marketing transactions are paid in advance, direct marketers have _____ advantages as compared to traditional retailers.
A. quantity discount
B. sales generation
C. seasonal
D. return policy
E. cash flow

13. Which is NOT a task usually associated with the fulfillment step in the direct marketing process?
A. deliver product information/sample
B. general leads
C. select media
D. order entry
E. shipping

14. Well-managed and effective fulfillment activities
A. increase returns.
B. minimize problems with regulatory groups.
C. add to the cost of returns.
D. decrease customer loyalty.
E. increase inventory costs.

15. When compared to other direct marketing tools, telemarketing is
A. better at reaching more contacts per hour.
B. less expensive per contact.
C. less intrusive.
D. more personal.
E. used less by large businesses such as GTE.

The remaining questions are designed to evaluate your ability to apply the text concepts.
16. Suppose one of the direct-response advertising cards included in a package of such cards sent to marketing managers is an offer from Prentice Hall about an opportunity to purchase a specific book. If the cost of having the card included was $5000, and the company received 1000 orders for the book, what is the cost per order?
A. $0.20
B. $0.40
C. $2.50
D. $4.00
E. $5.00

17. NordicTrack runs ads that contain a coupon offer for a free video tape explaining how the NordicTrack helps you lose weight and improve your health. The most likely immediate purpose for this ad is to
A. increase the ad's target audience.
B. determine how large the next mailer should be.
C. generate leads.
D. equate supply and demand.
E. create brand loyalty.

18. The process of making sure the flannel sheets that Eric ordered are delivered to him and are exactly the color and size he ordered is part of the _____ stage of direct marketing.
A. satisfaction
B. response
C. relationship maintenance
D. warm fuzzy
E. fulfillment

19. If Canine Dog Food company sends one promotional piece to owners of Great Danes and another one to owners of Cocker Spaniels, Canine is practicing what your text calls
A. multimarketing.
B. dual marketing.
C. double marketing.
D. multipositioning.
E. database marketing.

20. Balducci's fruit and vegetable store's catalog offering gourmet precooked meals is an example of a
A. retail merchandising catalog.
B. gourmet offering.
C. business catalog.
D. specialty catalog.
E. discount catalog.

21. If ABZ Company develops a three-page catalog of supplies for facsimile machines and sends it out to people via fax, the company is engaging in a form of
A. electronic mail.
B. direct mail.
C. media advertising.
D. informercial.
E. telemarketing.

22. Marketers anticipate that consumers will soon be able to call up an electronic mall on their computers, call up a list of products, request information about a specific sweater and see this sweater modeled by a fashion model on the computer screen, then order it, punch in a credit card number, and have it delivered the next day. This is an example of
A. use of videotex.
B. use of video catalogs.
C. interactive media use.
D. technomarketing.
E. maximarketing.

23. Which of the following is a direct marketing transaction? Sean needs a new raincoat. To satisfy this need he
A. borrows one from a friend.
B. purchases one from Target discount store.
C. orders one from his REI catalog.
D. buys one while shopping at Sam's Warehouse Club.
E. persuades his brother, a sales representative for Columbia outerwear, to buy one at cost for him from the wholesaler.

24. When a university develops a new degree program, they communicate the program's benefits only to those people who have a want for that specific knowledge. Your text calls this strategy
A. selective retention.
B. mass marketing.
C. fragment positioning.
D. precision targeting.
E. mini-marketing.

25. Louis received an E-mail message giving him a free 30-day trial use of a portable cellular telephone. He could respond through E-mail, the phone would arrive by Federal Express the next day and they would contact him after 30 days to determine his satisfaction. This is an example of what your book calls

A. a response.
B. the offer.
C. lead generation.
D. a proposal.
E. compensation.

26. The Body Shop has all customers sign a guest book while shopping in their store. According to your text, this would be an example of a _____ list.
A. response
B. retail
C. compiled
D. house
E. prospective

27. The state college launched a major promotion campaign asking anyone interested in on-line college courses to call a 1-800 number. They then used the _____ list generated as a database for direct marketing activities.
A. retail
B. response
C. house
D. compiled
E. audio

28. Russell wanted to mail company brochures to all the members of the Chamber of Commerce and all CEO's of companies with more than 50 employees. He realized there might be duplication so before the mailing he initiated a _____ process on the list.
A. sculpting
B. lead generation
C. merge-purge
D. complication
E. virus scan

29. Gina's first job was solicitation of computer sales by telephone. According to your text, Gina would be considered a
A. telemarketer.
B. direct mail salesperson.
C. database procurer.
D. media caller.
E. indirect marketer.

30. Author Susan Powter runs long-format advertising that looks like a talk show. This mass-media advertising is called a(n)
A. video catalog.
B. interactive media.
C. direct mail.
D. infomercial.
E. audiotext.

CHAPTER TWENTY-ONE
APPLICATIONS PROJECT

Purpose: To understand the applicability of the "selling process" to non-commercial endeavors.

Instructions: Finding the best career path for you will require experimentation and practice. To expedite, and fine tune the process, use the steps in the selling process for new customers as described on pages 657-663 of your text to promote yourself in the job market. If you already have a job with career potential use the "selling process for existing customers" on page 663.

Prospecting: (List all people/organizations that apply in each category.)
  Leads:

  Qualified Prospects:

Problem Solving: (What do the prospects need that you can provide.)

Approaching: (How will you make initial contact?)
  Cold call:

  Reference: (from a mutually-known source)

Presenting: (How do you rate against your competition.)
  Sales features: (personal strengths; experiences; skills.)

  Exclusive sales features: (competitive advantage)

  Resume: (do you have one? is it up-to-date? is it memorable? does it "sell" you?)

<u>Handling Objectives:</u> (Preparation is the key to success.)

Possible Objections

Your personal weaknesses.   Positive Response.
1.

2.

3.

<u>Closing the Sale:</u> (One way to "close" an interview is to recap the meeting, summarizing your
                 assets, as a lead-in to asking for the job.)

Summary of benefits to organization from hiring you:

<u>Follow Up:</u>
Thank you note/card: (Remind interviewer of anything unique discussed to refresh their
                 memory:)

     Your strengths:

     Organization's needs:

The following questions are designed to test your comprehension of marketing concepts and terminology.

1. Which of the following is NOT part of the personal selling process described in your text?
A. prospecting
B. problem solving
C. pioneering
D. approaching
E. follow up

2. Active listening, rephrasing, and testimonies are all tools that are particularly useful in the _____ stage of the personal selling process.
A. soliciting
B. approach
C. problem solving
D. prospecting
E. handling objections

3. Most professional salespeople feel that a good sales presentation involves about _____ percent talking and about _____ percent listening.
A. 90, 10
B. 75, 25
C. 25, 75
D. 0, 100
E. 100, 0

4. In personal selling, a stall is
A. a special selling booth at a trade show.
B. evasive behavior by a prospect to avoid or delay a buying decision.
C. a tactic used by salespeople to keep a client listening longer.
D. a tactic used by salespeople to postpone a potentially negative decision.
E. a special type of demonstration to display all of a product's features.

5. One of the major disadvantages of organizing a sales force by product line is
A. the hierarchical organization structure.
B. the vague chain of authority.
C. duplication of selling effort.
D. the skimpy knowledge base that the salesperson must work with.
E. too much information for one salesperson to handle.

6. _____ drives a pull strategy, while _____ drives a push strategy.
A. Sales promotion, advertising
B. Public relations, advertising
C. Advertising, public relations
D. Personal selling, advertising
E. Advertising, personal selling

7. Which of the following is NOT one of the major issues your text identifies as being important in sales management?
A. compensation
B. motivation
C. positioning
D. training
E. monitoring

8. If a sales representative is asked to provide information to the company about his or her personal assessments of such things as customer reactions to a new product or marketing campaign, the company is seeking what your text calls
A. qualitative reports.
B. quantitative reports.
C. call reports.
D. sales reports.
E. meeting logs.

9. Effective personal selling includes all of the following EXCEPT
A. two-way flow of communication.
B. identifying customer needs.
C. matching needs to firm's offering.
D. persuading customers to buy.
E. engaging mass media to deliver the messages.

10. Which of the following is NOT a strength of personal selling?
A. personal touch
B. flexibility
C. comparative cost
D. relationship-building potential
E. instant feedback

11. Partnering
A. excludes the salesperson.
B. increases channel conflict.
C. is the ultimate in relationship building.
D. is a declining business practice.
E. is not applicable to business-to-business selling.

12. _____ is a desirable quality in a salesperson.
A. Instability
B. Forcefulness
C. Quick temper
D. Sincerity
E. Negative attitude

13. Which of the following is not true when organizing a sales force along geographic lines?
A. reduced travel time
B. sales agents become territory managers
C. works best with diversified product mixes
D. works best with less technically sophisticated products
E. works best with a limited product line.

14. Compensation for salespeople
A. is the only important consideration once hired.
B. is not affected by educational background.
C. is universal by product line regardless of territory.
D. is determined independently of competition.
E. is dependent on the type of selling area.

15. The _____ the commission portion of a salesperson's compensation, the _____ motivated they may be to perform.
A. greater, more
B. greater, less
C. smaller, more
D. more structured, less
E. more unachievable, more

The remaining questions are designed to evaluate your ability to apply the text concepts.
16. Because Wilma was interested in buying a new set of Corelle cookware, she went to the store to talk to a sales clerk about buying a set if the price was resonable. To that sales clerk, Wilma is what your text would call
A. an order taker.
B. an order giver.
C. a prospect.
D. a prime shopper.
E. a qualified candidate.

17. A small Baptist church in rural South Carolina has no air conditioner, so it would be a(n) _____ for a person who sells air conditioners.
A. qualified prospect
B. ultimate consumer
C. lead
D. order giver
E. ordinal candidate

18. As part of its support program for the company's salespeople, Joseph asks the marketing research department to collect some detailed information about a particular company, including an in-depth analysis of that company and its performance. Joseph is requesting help with the _____ stage of personal selling.
A. prospect-study
B. presenting
C. closing
D. approaching
E. problem-solving

19. Steve is very careful to always be on time for all his sales appointments and dresses professionally. He also removes the earing from his nose before going out on sales calls. These actions show that Steve recognizes the importance of the _____ stage of the personal selling process.
A. presenting
B. prospecting
C. closing
D. approach
E. outset

20. Discovery Toy parties are generally run by independent agents selling Discovery's products directly to parents of end users. Discovery Toys is implementing
A. franchising.
B. direct selling.
C. agency marketing.
D. licensing.
E. functional selling

21. Tom won a free trip to Sydney, Australia, for himself and his wife for selling more office computer systems than anyone in his regional office in the previous years. Tom was the beneficiary of what your text would call a
A. creative commission program.
B. sales-incentive program.
C. salary-topping program.
D. salary bonus program.
E. motivational training program.

22. In his job as a salesperson for a major computer company, John carefully prepared a complete log of all of his phone calls and personal sales calls which he made each week in a report which he gave to his supervisor. Your text would call this report a
A. call report.
B. trip log.
C. sales log.
D. customer contact analysis.
E. sales report.

23. Paul knew his target market was informed on the benefits of his product. His next objective was to use his marketing communication mix to persuade his target audience to purchase. The best tool for Paul to accomplish this objective is
A. direct mail.
B. TV advertising.
C. personal selling.
D. publicity.
E. news release.

24. Before he could market himself in the "real world," John gathered information on all the companies where he would like to work. According to your text, this search for potential employers is called
A. direct marketing.
B. prospecting.
C. closing.
D. presenting.
E. approaching.

25. Bud Dry promotes their product to people over the legal drinking age who like beer. Tom is 31 and is a Budweiser drinker. Tom would be a(n) _____ for the promoters of Bud Dry.
A. qualified prospect
B. referral lead
C. order giver
D. gatekeeper
E. approach

26. Eager to earn his commission in his new job selling copiers, Damien drove up and down main street making sales calls on unqualified prospects without an appointment. This type of approach is called
A. prospecting.
B. a referral.
C. a mission call.
D. a cold call.
E. closed call.

27. After she overcame the objections, Catherine made a T chart with her prospect. Together, they listed all the advantages of buying her new product on one side, the disadvantages on the other. When the customer saw the long list of benefits, she agreed to make the purchase. This result proved Catherine's T chart had done a good job of
A. referral trial.
B. cold calling.
C. lead generation.
D. follow up.
E. closing.

28. After closing on Paul and Carol's new house, their Realtor sent flowers to thank them on moving day. This is considered part of the selling process known as
A. closing.
B. follow up.
C. approach.
D. handling objections.
E. problem solving.

29. Marshall was hired by Cellular One with the agreement that he would sign up 50 new customers a month. According to your text, this sales objective is called
A. territory target.
B. sales quota.
C. closing quota.
D. discount.
E. commission.

30. Madeline wanted to improve her chances of getting a sales job after graduation. She was advised to improve her _____ skills, one of a salesperson's most important tools.
A. aggressive persuasion.
B. confrontation escalation.
C. ignore and disclaim.
D. active listening.
E. bait and switch.

CHAPTER TWENTY-TWO
EXAM PRACTICE QUESTIONS

The following questions are designed to test your comprehension of marketing concepts and terminology.

1. The process of achieving a company's desired goals through the most efficient use of resources and strategies is called
A. management.
B. planning.
C. strategy.
D. marketing.
E. communication.

2. Getting the best possible results from available resources is referred to as
A. maximization.
B. extension.
C. elasticity.
D. leverage.
E. minimization.

3. Comparing numbers by putting them on the same scale, often using 100 as the base or average number, is called
A. indexing.
B. benchmarking.
C. average analysis.
D. scale settling.
E. megascaling.

4. Marketing costs include expenditures to all of the following EXCEPT
A. determining the needs of the market.
B. making products available.
C. communication with customers.
D. maintaining production equipment.
E. marketing administration and overhead.

5. Copytesting is evaluating
A. copy internally by testing for consistency, memorability, and directness.
B. the reproductive quality of an advertisement.
C. advertising in terms of audience recall, recognition and understanding.
D. the headline and layout of an advertisement for internal consistency.
E. the headline and body copy of an advertisement for internal consistency.

6. A product's operating margin is
A. the amount of revenue a product brings in as a ratio of total company sales.
B. the difference between a product's production cost and advertising costs.
C. a product's costs as a percentage of total company's costs.
D. the difference between the cost of a product and its selling price.
E. a measure of marketing share.

7. As outlined in your text, one of the keys to good management is
A. more internal competition.
B. better internal communication.
C. less sharing of information.
D. increase seriousness.
E. ambiguity.

8. Making predictions based on the assumption that a past trend will continue into the future is called
A. extension.
B. histrionics.
C. benchmarking.
D. indexing.
E. extrapolation.

9. All of the following apply to the concept of stretch EXCEPT
A. ambition exceeds present resources.
B. it is a strategic discipline.
C. it is the same as fit.
D. encourages companies to come up with new ideas.
E. opens new ways of creating value for the customer.

10. One of the most important and stressful working relationships is between "inside" marketing and
A. salespeople.
B. customers.
C. competitors.
D. distribution.
E. switchables.

11. Which of the following is a tactic to assist with timing decisions?
A. stretch
B. flow charts
C. maneuvering
D. leverage
E. process teams

12.
Marketing management includes
A. achievement of company goals.
B. efficient use of resources.
C. planning the marketing mix.
D. control and evaluation procedures.
E. all of the above.

13. Budgeting
A. consists of informal speculation.
B. is not applicable/useful to non-profit organizations.
C. relies on forecast.

D. has no impact on staff attitude and moral.

E. deals exclusively with resource allocation.

14. Brand proliferation

A. results in a more efficient spread of resources.

B. reduces the number of brands marketed.

C. makes individual brands stronger.

D. dilutes marketing forces.

E. is part of market share analysis.

15. Once a product/service's marketing mix has been evaluated, a _____ analysis must be conducted to determine operating and profit margins.

A. trend

B. inventory

C. advertising

D. brand

E. profitability

The remaining questions are designed to evaluate your ability to apply the text concepts.

16. Saturn's approach to providing a fixed price with lots of service and personal attention is based on the "future concept of marketing" which focuses on

A. volume sales.

B. salary-plus-commission.

C. relationship building.

D. profit margins.

E. customer contact.

17. In order for Actibath to introduce carbonated bath tablets with moisturizers before Christmas, the marketing department had to coordinate a number of activities. It most likely used _____ to determine which activity would take the longest, and therefore needed to begun immediately to avoid holding up everything else.

A. CPM

B. DMZ

C. indexing

D. trend analysis

E. extrapolation

18. XYZ Company made some major changes in the way the company was organized, including changing some work units into process teams, where group of workers work together to complete a whole piece of work. Job content was switched from single task to multidimensional work with many different components, and employees were asked to shift from following orders to devising and regulating their own work procedures. XYZ Company's actions are examples of what your text calls

A. holistic management.

B. task holition.

C. global redefinition.

D. retrofitting.

E. reengineering.

19. Whenever commercials come on his TV set, Zach automatically switches to other channels to see what else is on. He doesn't switch back until he thinks the commercials are over. Zach is practicing what advertisers call
A. switching behavior.
B. zipping.
C. zapping.
D. errant viewing.
E. sporadic viewing.

20. Cambell Soup Company had an external management team come in to determine which product, person, or function added value to the company's brand and to determine the overall efficiency and effectiveness of its marketing programs. In doing this, Cambell was conducting
A. a system analysis.
B. a market review.
C. a brand review.
D. a marketing audit.
E. a value inspection.

21. Sue started her business with no resources, but she knew what customers wanted and always had aspirations beyond her resources. Her strategic use of _____ made her a successful.
A. achievement
B. resource extension
C. stretch
D. omnipotence
E. derivation

22. Eric prerecords all sports games from his television, then watches them later in the day so that he doesn't have to watch the commercials. He just puts the videocassette on fast-forward when the commercials are on. Eric is doing what advertisers call
A. zipping.
B. zapping.
C. errant viewing.
D. skimming.
E. periodic viewing.

23. Brian studied the practices that made other Karate schools successful. He then adjusted his marketing mix in order to achieve equal or better results. Brian was
A. prospecting.
B. stretching.
C. flow charting.
D. benchmarking.
E. indexing.

24. Dave's Donuts needed a quick way of predicting future demand. They developed a _____ by extrapolating from last year's sales to calculate sales growth for the next year.
A. flow chart
B. benchmark
C. PERT chart
D. index abbreviation
E. trend analysis

25. Before reporting on his marketing plan's success at the stockholders annual meeting, Ben must calculate the company's percentage of sales in their particular industry. According to you text, this concept is called
A. market share analysis.
B. indexing.
C. benchmarking.
D. trend analysis.
E. precision targeting.

26. Jeff sold the entire shelf of 30 cans of tennis balls 52 times in 1994. Compared with the industry average for on-site pro shops of 15 cans/week, Jeff's _____ was excellent.
A. operational margin
B. inventory turnover
C. return on investment
D. market share
E. copytesting

27. To be a successful manager you will need
A. a strict apposition to change.
B. a strong selling orientation.
C. an adversarial relationship with the customer.
D. the flexibility to adopt to opportunities.
E. to be ignorant of environmental threats.

28. The new sales manager had the company's vision printed on all sales brochures, made into a plaque for the showroom, and explained in a letter to existing customers. However, the implementation of the vision was unsuccessful because she forgot to clearly communicate its importance to
A. the competitors.
B. the government.
C. the employees.
D. the vendors.
E. the general public.

29. Which of the following is NOT an example of a marketing audit?
A. Nike hires a consultant to evaluate their company.
B. GM employees assess the effectiveness on the firm's internal marketing strategy.
C. Caterpillar asks industry experts to determine if their sales force is adequate.
D. Keebler blames sagging sales on the elves and fires them.
E. Coke participates in a joint venture with a Russian marketing firm to evaluate Coke's current marketing presence and discover growth opportunities.

30. LMN enterprises has experienced market share decreases of more than 10% over the past three years. This most likely indicates a problem with
A. the economy.
B. the PERT chart.
C. the company's marketing plan.
D. the company's index.
E. the competition.

CHAPTER ONE
ANSWERS

1.E	11.B	21.B
2.E	12.C	22.A
3.B	13.A	23.E
4.E	14.C	24.B
5.B	15.D	25.A
6.B	16.A	26.A
7.C	17.E	27.A
8.D	18.C	28.B
9.C	19.D	29.A
10.E	20.D	30.D

CHAPTER TWO
ANSWERS

1.C	11.B	21.A
2.E	12.B	22.C
3.D	13.D	23.A
4.A	14.D	24.B
5.A	15.D	25.A
6.D	16.B	26.A
7.C	17.C	27.E
8.A	18.A	28.B
9.E	19.C	29.D
10.C	20.B	30.E

CHAPTER THREE
ANSWERS

1.A	11.E	21.C
2.A	12.D	22.B
3.A	13.C	23.B
4.A	14.E	24.B
5.B	15.A	25.A
6.D	16.E	26.B
7.C	17.A	27.E
8.B	18.A	28.D
9.C	19.C	29.B
10.A	20.E	30.A

CHAPTER FOUR
ANSWERS

1.A	11.B	21.A
2.E	12.E	22.D
3.C	13.B	23.C
4.C	14.C	24.B
5.A	15.A	25.D
6.B	16.B	26.E
7.D	17.A	27.B
8.C	18.E	28.A
9.B	19.C	29.C
10.A	20.C	30.A

CHAPTER FIVE
ANSWERS

1.C	11.D	21.D
2.C	12.A	22.E
3.D	13.E	23.E
4.A	14.D	24.A
5.A	15.E	25.A
6.C	16.C	26.B
7.A	17.A	27.C
8.C	18.B	28.D
9.C	19.E	29.A
10.B	20.B	30.B

CHAPTER SIX
ANSWERS

1.A	11.D	21.A
2.C	12.B	22.E
3.C	13.A	23.B
4.C	14.D	24.B
5.E	15.D	25.B
6.E	16.D	26.C
7.E	17.B	27.E
8.A	18.D	28.A
9.E	19.B	29.D
10.A	20.C	30.C

CHAPTER SEVEN
ANSWERS

1.A	11.D	21.A
2.E	12.A	22.E
3.C	13.D	23.D
4.E	14.D	24.B
5.C	15.B	25.C
6.D	16.D	26.C
7.E	17.D	27.E
8.E	18.D	28.A
9.D	19.D	29.A
10.A	20.E	30.C

CHAPTER EIGHT
ANSWERS

1.D	11.B	21.D
2.B	12.D	22.B
3.C	13.B	23.A
4.D	14.C	24.D
5.C	15.D	25.C
6.C	16.C	26.D
7.A	17.D	27.B
8.A	18.E	28.B
9.B	19.A	29.D
10.E	20.D	30.D

CHAPTER NINE
ANSWERS

1.B	11.C	21.B
2.E	12.A	22.D
3.B	13.C	23.D
4.C	14.B	24.C
5.B	15.B	25.D
6.A	16.E	26.E
7.D	17.E	27.E
8.A	18.D	28.C
9.B	19.C	29.E
10.D	20.A	30.A

CHAPTER TEN
ANSWERS

1.B	11.B	21.C
2.D	12.A	22.B
3.B	13.D	23.A
4.E	14.C	24.A
5.D	15.C	25.B
6.B	16.B	26.A
7.A	17.A	27.D
8.B	18.C	28.C
9.C	19.C	29.D
10.D	20.D	30.E

CHAPTER ELEVEN
ANSWERS

1.C	11.A	21.B
2.B	12.B	22.B
3.E	13.C	23.C
4.C	14.A	24.B
5.E	15.B	25.D
6.E	16.A	26.E
7.D	17.E	27.D
8.C	18.E	28.B
9.D	19.B	29.A
10.C	20.A	30.E

CHAPTER TWELVE
ANSWERS

1.A	11.E	21.A
2.E	12.E	22.A
3.B	13.B	23.B
4.E	14.C	24.C
5.E	15.B	25.A
6.A	16.A	26.E
7.D	17.D	27.E
8.B	18.D	28.C
9.D	19.E	29.D
10.B	20.B	30.E

CHAPTER THIRTEEN
ANSWERS

1.C	11.B	21.D
2.E	12.A	22.E
3.D	13.E	23.E
4.A	14.C	24.A
5.D	15.B	25.C
6.D	16.D	26.D
7.A	17.B	27.B
8.B	18.D	28.A
9.B	19.E	29.C
10.D	20.E	30.B

CHAPTER FOURTEEN
ANSWERS

1.A	11.C	21.B
2.C	12.C	22.E
3.C	13.A	23.D
4.B	14.B	24.E
5.D	15.E	25.A
6.A	16.D	26.B
7.B	17.B	27.C
8.C	18.C	28.B
9.D	19.C	29.E
10.A	20.C	30.D

CHAPTER FIFTEEN
ANSWERS

1.A	11.B	21.D
2.A	12.C	22.D
3.D	13.D	23.B
4.E	14.D	24.D
5.A	15.B	25.E
6.A	16.B	26.A
7.A	17.E	27.B
8.D	18.A	28.A
9.A	19.C	29.B
10.D	20.D	30.E

CHAPTER SIXTEEN
ANSWERS

1.E	11.A	21.C
2.A	12.C	22.B
3.B	13.C	23.C
4.B	14.D	24.E
5.A	15.E	25.B
6.B	16.E	26.A
7.A	17.D	27.C
8.E	18.A	28.D
9.B	19.D	29.E
10.E	20.B	30.A

CHAPTER SEVENTEEN
ANSWERS

1.A	11.B	21.E
2.A	12.A	22.A
3.C	13.C	23.D
4.A	14.E	24.B
5.A	15.D	25.E
6.C	16.C	26.A
7.A	17.D	27.E
8.D	18.B	28.B
9.C	19.B	29.A
10.E	20.D	30.D

CHAPTER EIGHTEEN
ANSWERS

1.A	11.A	21.D
2.D	12.E	22.B
3.A	13.D	23.B
4.D	14.B	24.A
5.E	15.A	25.E
6.D	16.B	26.C
7.C	17.D	27.D
8.D	18.A	28.B
9.C	19.D	29.C
10.C	20.E	30.A

CHAPTER NINETEEN
ANSWERS

1.C	11.E	21.C
2.A	12.D	22.B
3.A	13.B	23.B
4.B	14.C	24.A
5.D	15.E	25.B
6.B	16.D	26.D
7.E	17.B	27.E
8.C	18.E	28.C
9.C	19.A	29.A
10.A	20.B	30.E

CHAPTER TWENTY
ANSWERS

1.A	11.A	21.E
2.C	12.E	22.C
3.A	13.C	23.C
4.E	14.B	24.D
5.A	15.D	25.B
6.A	16.E	26.D
7.D	17.C	27.B
8.D	18.E	28.C
9.B	19.E	29.A
10.E	20.D	30.D

CHAPTER TWENTY-ONE
ANSWERS

1.C	11.C	21.B
2.E	12.D	22.A
3.C	13.C	23.C
4.B	14.E	24.B
5.C	15.A	25.A
6.E	16.C	26.D
7.C	17.C	27.E
8.A	18.E	28.B
9.E	19.D	29.B
10.C	20.B	30.D

CHAPTER TWENTY-TWO
ANSWERS

1.A	11.B	21.C
2.D	12.E	22.A
3.A	13.C	23.D
4.D	14.D	24.E
5.C	15.E	25.A
6.D	16.C	26.B
7.B	17.A	27.D
8.E	18.E	28.C
9.C	19.C	29.D
10.A	20.D	30.C